Praise for *F*

"Andrea Clarke has given us such a gift with this book. She shows us how to turn vulnerability into a strength, adversity into resilience and the rapidly changing challenges of a modern work world into opportunities to seize. And she does so with an engaging, hilarious and crisp to-the-point writing style that makes you feel like you are chatting with her over a coffee. It is rare for me not to be able to put a book down, but that was my experience with *Future Fit*. And as I navigate my career or just need a boost of confidence, I'll rely on her wise words for years to come."

Laura Capps, Speechwriter for President Bill Clinton

"Overwhelmingly refreshing in insight and simplicity, Andrea provides a roadmap for the confusion of the eternal 'future of work' question, through thrilling and brilliant storytelling. Funny, overwhelmingly honest and relatable, I found this book a satisfying and entertaining read on feeling more in control of the future to come."

Alicia Stephenson, Director, Generational Dynamics, Incorp

"Andrea takes us on a journey where we realise that we own our future and it's time to take action and not be a bystander. *Future Fit* equips you with enough exercises for a thriving career for you, and those who role-model your behaviours. It's a true force multiplier to embrace uncertainty."

Dominic Price, Futurist, Atlassian

"This is truly an incredible read for CEOs and leaders who know that closing the human skills gap will spark the innovation needed to stay competitive and pursue new market opportunities. Andrea takes readers on a journey that helps build comfort and excitement about the future of work."

Jacinta Jones, Chief Customer Officer, RollitSuper

"As a foreign correspondent and in-demand corporate trainer, Andrea has a unique insight into how businesses around the world operate. She's observed leaders who've looked ahead, swiftly adapted and succeeded as a result. This book is a clear guide of how it's done. It's clever and fast-paced. *Future Fit* is for anyone who doesn't want to get left behind."

Mia Greves, Corporate Communication Professional

"Clarke's inspiring and passionate storytelling combines practical and actionable advice for women and men that you won't be able to put down."

Tim Fawcett, Head of Government Affairs, Cisco

"Many parents ask me what they can do to help guide their children to future opportunities. From now on I'm going to tell them to read *Future Fit*. The future can be created, and Andrea's work neatly summarises the keys to future success."

Dr Catherine Ball, Scientist and Entrepreneur

In *Future Fit*, Andrea Clarke tells not just her story but also tells a story of resilience, of skill acquisition and of how to deal with intimidating situations in the workforce. Here is a book of practical advice on how to navigate the future of work when you don't quite know what the future holds."

Bernard Salt AM, The Demographics Group

FUTURE

Fit

How to Stay Relevant and Competitive in the **Future of Work**

ANDREA CLARKE

First published in 2019 by Major Street Publishing Pty Ltd
PO Box 106, Highett, Vic. 3190
E: info@majorstreet.com.au
W: majorstreet.com.au
M: +61 421 707 983

Quantity sales. Special discounts are available on quantity purchases by corporations, associations and others. For details, contact Lesley Williams using the contact details above.

Individual sales. Major Street publications are available through most bookstores. They can also be ordered directly from Major Street's online bookstore at www.majorstreet.com.au.

Orders for university textbook/course adoption use. For orders of this nature, please contact Lesley Williams using the contact details above.

The moral rights of the author have been asserted.

 A catalogue record for this book is available from the National Library of Australia

ISBN: 978-0-6484100-7-2

Internal design by Production Works
Cover design by Sarah Cronin, Bluehaus Designs
Cover photo by Ross Coffey
Printed in Australia by Ovato, an Accredited ISO AS/NZS 14001:2004 Environmental Management System Printer.

10 9 8 7 6 5 4 3 2 1

Disclaimer: The material in this publication is in the nature of general comment only, and neither purports nor intends to be advice. Readers should not act on the basis of any matter in this publication without considering (and if appropriate taking) professional advice with due regard to their own particular circumstances. The author and publisher expressly disclaim all and any liability to any person, whether a purchaser of this publication or not, in respect of anything and the consequences of anything done or omitted to be done by any such person in reliance, whether whole or partial, upon the whole or any part of the contents of this publication.

Contents

Acknowledgements

Working on *Future Fit* has been an absolute delight.

I would like to thank all of those who helped me formulate, write, delete and sharpen every part of it. Specifically, the initial conversations that helped me shape this idea – thank you to Steve Smorgon in Melbourne and Eric Delabarre in Los Angeles. Lesley Williams, thank you for backing my idea from the starting line. Bernard Salt, thank you for your instant support, encouragement and contribution to this and every idea I have. To the entire CareerCEO community and crew including my two principal facilitators and personal oversight committee, Belinda Wall and Jennifer Adams – thank you for your extraordinary talents, your candid thoughts, keeping me in check and helping me build such a meaningful business. Thank you to my outstandingly creative neighbour, Sarah Cronin. Anthea Becke, thank you for running my life and being such a wonderful support. To my neighbours, pilates instructors, friends and colleagues who caught me when I was my own content vortex and was not capable of alternative conversations – I hope it all makes sense now.

The idea for this book came out of a very confusing session on blockchain, so to my Silicon Valley travel pal, Philippa Huxley, thank you for being as excited about the future of work as I am – I still don't know what blockchain is so can you explain it to me one more time...?

My only intention with this book is to get you thinking.

Foreword

Get comfortable with the idea of change

In some ways it is the biggest question of our time in history. How do I remain relevant in a rapidly changing world and workplace? Some say the answer is education; others say it is being adaptable and resilient. I think the development of 'people skills' is an important part of the whole remaining-relevant story.

It's almost as if modern workers, and employers, are looking for a single quality to remaining relevant. Yet, as with most things in life, maybe the answer is more complex. What if the way to make workers relevant to the future of work is different for every worker? This more nuanced approach would require an understanding of the bigger forces shaping society as well as a kind of manual to help workers remain focused on how to be fit for the future of work.

Let's begin by looking at how the world of work, and the world more generally, has changed and is changing. From there we'll discuss solutions and strategies to overcoming skill gaps. What workers really need is an understanding of the bigger picture, evidence of the skills that might be needed in the future, and practical advice about how to manage all-too-familiar workplace situations.

How has the world of work changed?

It seems like the pace of social and economic change has quickened over the last decade, and especially in Australia. The local car-making industry, for example, has been reimagined by globalisation of the manufacturing process. The governance and the ethics of the banking industry have come under intense scrutiny, prompting calls for a change in culture and in regulation.

The mining industry is now less labour-intensive than it was even a decade ago; it has evolved into a highly mechanised transport and logistics business. These bigger-picture forces have also applied to agribusiness, although in this sector the immediate focus seems to have been the need for economies of scale via farm aggregation.

Profound social and technological change is evident across most facets of modern life. The use of cash – actually handling notes – seems 'messy' and less hygienic than clinically tapping payment, as we like to do today. The beloved ink-ridden newspaper – especially the broadsheet variety – has been weakened, and some say terminally so, by the rise of online news sources.

And then there is the landline which is, apparently, all but dead. (Note to today's teenagers: a landline is a telephone handset that was attached by a line fixed to a wall or to a skirting board within the family home. No, really.)

Postal mail, let alone truly archaic concepts like the aerogramme and the telegram, as well as fax machines and even answering machines have been consigned to a period of time with a start date and an end date. Black and white television might have started in Australia in 1956 but it began to be superseded with the arrival of colour TV from 1975 onwards.

No one queried the effects of this new technological marvel on the television-making workforce at the time, but perhaps this was because it was seen as an exciting new product. No one was 'disrupted' by colour television, and indeed its arrival merely prompted a new all-round heightened consumerism.

Music was once committed to pressed vinyl, then it was committed to cassette tape, then to compact disk (CD) and from there it was streamed and shared as it is today. The entire transition of the way music was consumed took place between the 1980s and the early 2000s. And yet its effects have been wider and more substantive than, say, the introduction of colour television.

Artists needed to realign their management interests and creative output away from recording companies (such as EMI) and towards global technology businesses (such as Apple). The transition wasn't neat and efficient; it played out messily and over a decade or more. Some artists seized the moment whereas others proved to be laggards.

But eventually the pathway becomes clear. Streamed music is a better product – meaning it is more convenient and accessible – than a vinyl record. Bigger farms offer better economies of scale than smaller farms. Cars made in China can be produced and shipped to Australia more cheaply than they can be manufactured in Australia. And tapping a credit card is a faster and more frictionless method of conducting a transaction than accessing, carrying and passing over the required amount of cash. I suspect that not only has the landline disappeared from the family home but so too has the plastic ice-cream bucket with stored coins.

The point of this is that 'change' has been part of the way we have lived and worked for a generation or more. But something changed in the way things change, about a decade ago. The world is now more globally connected via trade. Corporations are even more inclined to take on a global perspective: what works in America is likely to work in Australia or the UK, for example. Cheap air travel means that the middle class in both the West and in developing countries can and do travel.

Consumers and workers are increasingly exposed to wider influences from leading economies such as those of the US, Japan, Europe and China.

The Chinese middle class aspire to elements of the Western lifestyle including owning high-end branded goods, drinking red wine, eating dairy products and even beef. New Yorkers discerningly eat sushi just as the average Australian can now master chopsticks. In a global world where ideas, fashion, technology and corporations move seamlessly from place to place it is logical that both the present and the future belong to the skilled, to the agile and to the resilient.

Change has always been part of everyday life. The difference today is that the pace of change has quickened, and its impacts are wider reaching. The demise of the car-making industry in Australia created unemployment among those with tool-making skills but it accelerated demand for transportation, logistics and warehousing functionalities.

There are fewer farm labourers today than there were a generation ago but there is greater demand for niche growers (consider the demand for bok choy and pak choi, for example) and for value-added processing. It is also possible that in the future Australian farm produce could be shipped fresh via expanded regional airports into Chinese markets as is currently the case at Toowoomba's Wellcamp airport.

Between the last two Australian censuses the job that lost most workers was the role of secretary, down 19,000 positions. The reason is clear enough. Over the last decade, senior management has learnt how to type. Even the Chief Executive Officer and the Chairman of the board of directors now communicate via self-typed email. There is no need for a memorandum to be dictated, *Mad Men* style, to a transcribing secretary.

As a consequence, secretaries have had to reinvent themselves as 'office managers' where they draw upon their typing skills, their IT knowledge, their HR expertise and their corporate experience to manage and to deliver the outcome of an efficient and an inspired workforce.

Overcoming the skill gaps

What is required of the secretary is the same as what is required of the retrenched tool-maker. They both need access to a vast and evolving job market that offers work as an office manager or perhaps as a warehouse manager or forklift driver. But there is something else that is required of these displaced workers and that is an inherent willingness to be retrained, as well as the social skills and the self-confidence to pitch for available work. This is not easy for some people and especially for those who have been in long-term jobs.

It is understandable that displaced secretaries as well as retrenched car-manufacturing workers might feel resentful about losing their jobs. But this is part of the overall challenge of reinventing yourself to surf the waves of change rather than to wallow and be swamped by the forces of change. These changes are being driven by global forces and by the fundamental consumer desire to live a better life, to live a frictionless life, a life that offers better value-for-money access to consumer goods and experiences. These are unstoppable forces.

Your role in this wider world of change is to remain upbeat, to retain social connections, to hone skills, to scan the horizon for opportunities and threats, and to understand that no technology, no workplace, no enterprise, no management structure can last indefinitely.

At various points, perhaps even at numerous points, in your working life you will have to reinvent yourself or at the very least change the basis upon which you earn a living. It is unrealistic to rail against the forces of change. You need to get comfortable with change. You need to see how others have managed this process and to extract learnings and lessons.

And who better to tell you a powerful story of reinvention than former Washington D.C. television news correspondent, humanitarian aid worker and expert media trainer Andrea Clarke, who has built a nationwide corporate training business?

In *Future Fit* Clarke tells not just her own heart-pounding, gritty and at times laugh-out-loud funny story, but she also tells a story of extraordinary resilience, of skill acquisition and of how to deal with intimidating situations and people in today's workforce. Here is a book of practical advice on how to navigate the future of work when you don't quite know precisely what the future holds.

Bernard Salt AM

Preface

When robots 'take our jobs', what do we have left? A remarkable opportunity to be more 'human' than ever before. I believe firmly that the future of work is about being more connected to ourselves, our purpose and our power to do more meaningful work – everything that cannot be automated. It's not about the technology – it's about how we want to live, work and contribute to our communities.

As artificial intelligence is adopted into the workplace and traditional employee arrangements transform, we're heading for a far looser, less structured work arena. For organisations, it means reimagining talent models and redefining business practices. For employees, it means understanding that the responsibility for finding, securing and delivering work is shifting to the individual in ways we have not seen before. While the fault line is clear, so is the opportunity: those who take 'human skills' to the next level will be powerfully differentiated in a dynamic new market. There is a multitude of human skills, but I have chosen to focus on eight: reputation capital, communication, adaptability, creativity, networking, leadership, problem solving and continuous learning. If we want to stay competitive, grow and prosper in our chosen fields then we need to invest in ways to develop these and take them to the next level, because they will each need to be applied in new ways as we move into a new environment.

This book will help equip you with a new kind of job security – the security we create for ourselves by investing in our own capability. I'm going to explain and explore the tactical tools that will help you become invaluable to your current employer, capture emerging roles across your sector and create roles that may never be advertised on a job seeker website. These eight human skills will help us all lean towards change and become an asset to ourselves and the company we work for, instead of a liability. I'll help you avoid the fault lines, identify what you want to excel at and sharpen up your view of the workplace to see the vast opportunity that disruption presents to all of us. I'll help you be the person who is 'fit and able', regardless of the environment.

The trademark of my career so far has been not just showing up, but keeping up with change in myself and the businesses which I have been a part of: job loss when I least expected it, working in an industry that largely failed to adapt to shifting audience trends in real time, and navigating the sharp edges of starting a small consultancy business. In each career transition, there have been no safety nets. There has only been one constant – investing in myself to consistently add value to a business, maintain currency in the market and evolve intellectually.

Staying 'Future Fit' was driven by my own desire for growth. As it turns out, those skills which I have been delivering and teaching to emerging leaders now take on more meaning – they're the skills that can help us all accelerate into a future of work where we are more exposed and more responsible for our own path.

My wake-up call to staying Future Fit happened while I was on assignment in Iraq, which is where I want to take you now...

Andrea Clarke
www.careerceo.com.au

Bombshell in Baghdad

"Choose courage over comfort. And choose the great adventure of being both brave and afraid, at the exact same time." —BRENE BROWN

"Stand by for a rapid descent!"

It's not a phrase you ever dream of hearing, but it's what I heard early in the morning of 28 September 2008 when I found myself sitting halfway down from the cockpit of a UN charter jet, flying into a war zone over Baghdad, Iraq. The adrenalin surging through me was explosive, when the 30-seat plane suddenly banked hard to the left and began a free-fall nosedive towards the scorching sands of the Iraqi desert.

I wish I could say the experience forced me to face some profound epiphany about life or our purpose on this planet, but it didn't. My only reaction was to let out a scream of "Oh my God!", as I prepared myself for the distinct possibility of a fiery death in a plane crash over Iraq.

Now, here's the thing about an aircraft in the middle of a nosedive from 20,000 feet, the sound of the engine shifting gears to speed up and slow down is deeply alarming. This was no standard commercial flight, where the pilot's job was to make the journey as smooth as possible. I was the only passenger on the dangerous hop from Amman, Jordan to Baghdad, but at no time on this flight did the pilot offer words of reassurance, which was seriously disconcerting.

With only the smooth sound of John Mayer playing through my headphones and my laser-focused pilot in front of me for company, I felt so alone. I watched the desert rush towards us and suddenly realised how a skydiver must feel, if the parachute fails to open. What I found strange (other than the obvious) was where a person's mind races when faced with such an unnerving experience. I found myself captivated by the lines that divided up the desert below. I was a sky-high witness to a desert puzzle. There I was, screaming vertically towards an active war zone, and I was curious about lines in the sand.

I started to reflect...

Under normal circumstances, I'm not even close to being afraid of flying. Quite the contrary: I love it. I grew up flying with my dad on many weekends and school holidays when I was a kid. My father ran a rapidly expanding business involving trucking haulage, so having a light aircraft was more of a necessity than a luxury for him in the early 1980s, when he needed to cover extreme distances around regional Queensland. Dad's first plane was a Cessna 172 – an American, four-seat, single-engine, high-wing, fixed-wing aircraft. Since we were too young to sit up front, my two sisters and I sat in the back seat, obeying Dad's one rule "no shenanigans". If we could have only followed this rule in life on the ground, I'm sure we would have made our parents (and each other) a lot happier.

A few years later Dad upgraded to a Cessna 182, before finally settling on the Cessna 210, to accommodate the increasing luggage of his three teenage daughters. ("Only pack what you can carry" was a routine instruction, little did I know then that it would turn out to be a life mantra.)

We loved the new plane, not because of the size of it or because Dad flew it himself across the Pacific Ocean from Hawaii. We loved it because the wheels retracted after take-off. We all felt a deep sense of ease and adventure with flying, so I've never really shared the common fear of commercial aviation. That being said, nor had I ever been a passenger flying over a heavily monitored military airspace, dropping 20,000 feet in a matter of minutes.

Back to Baghdad

At the time of my descent, Baghdad International was the most heavily defended airport in the world. While I knew that – and thank God it was – there was still plenty to be concerned about. If you wanted to land in Baghdad in one piece, the landing must resemble a skydiving 'halo drop' – (a high altitude – low opening) jump from 25,000 feet – in an attempt to remain undetected. Insurgents were stationed right outside the protected airspace, armed with surface-to-air missiles, and perfectly willing and able to blow up civilian or military aircraft with a single shot.

The anxiety of the situation was real, so I switched to a Navy SEAL 'box' breathing technique to slow my heart rate – breathe in for four seconds, hold for four seconds and then exhale for four seconds. It's incredibly simple and very powerful. When we take deliberate control over our breathing, we control our nervous system to bleed off excess stress. Beyond the obvious benefit of reducing angst, when you stack this with a positive vocal mantra (in this case: "I am completely safe") it allows you to focus and conserve energy instead of haemorrhaging adrenalin that you'll likely need.

As the ground raced up towards us and I feared the worst, I was suddenly pulled to the left. In an expert simultaneous manoeuvre, which made me think my pilot was a retired fighter pilot or a fighter pilot who was moonlighting for the UN, the pilot hit the air brakes and steered the aircraft into a tight downward spiral.

Normal landings can take miles to execute, but in a war zone you don't have the luxury or the time. Think of it this way: landing in such a small zone would be similar to trying to land your plane into a tall glass of water. Having a basic understanding of aviation, I knew that the spiral technique was the only way to come out of a nosedive without leaving the protected airspace.

When the spiralling moves finally ended, which felt like the hard banking of a roller coaster ride at an amusement park, my pilot pulled out of the rotation, levelled the nose of the aircraft and started our final approach. This might sound crazy, but final approach was more dangerous than nosediving 20,000 feet. At this airspeed, which was around 180 knots, we were at our most vulnerable. The faster the speed, the harder it is to hit us with a missile. So we were a slow-moving duck at the start of hunting season. If you're going to land at the world's most protected but dangerous airport ideally you do it as fast as possible.

My adrenalin levels were off the charts. I was instantly exhausted, as if I'd done a two-hour sprint on a treadmill. Then I heard the landing gear doors opening and the wheels lock into place. The screeching of the tyres as they hit the tarmac was the most comforting sound of this whole experience. We had made it. My father used to say any landing is a good landing, but this wasn't any landing. This was only the starting blocks of a very dangerous assignment.

Relief, momentarily

Baghdad International Airport had very strict rules about landing aircraft. Planes were not allowed to get too close to the terminal for a laundry list of terror-related reasons. We pulled to a stop over 100 metres away from the terminal. The "I'm safe now" relief of touchdown was swiftly replaced with the harsh reality of the situation: we were smack bang in the middle of an active war zone. Safety is a relative term when you're standing on the tarmac, exposed to sniper fire. I'm 'safe', you know, compared to being embedded with a platoon of US Marines in the Iraqi province of Al Anbar, for example!

When the pilot finally cracked open the door, I felt a wave of searing desert heat roll through the empty cabin and hit me in the face. "Ah, yes... dry heat, thank God", I remember thinking to myself and allowing my thoughts to wander... I cannot stand humidity. Everything is 100% harder in wet heat. A few years earlier, while in Cambodia with a non-profit group, I was shooting a story for CNN on unexploded land mines (which the mine-hunters subsequently found and enthusiastically exploded for my story), when I came to accept that I was far less fun in humidity. When the air is so dense it feels like a sauna and I lose part of my upbeat personality. I guess that makes me normal. I know this about myself. So, for the most part, I'm happy to be met with dry heat. Scared, but happy in this micro-window of a moment.

I took the deepest breath on personal record and snapped my seat belt free. The pilot extracted himself out of his seat. He looked like he'd had a rough time of it as well. His shirt was loosely tucked in and he looked tired. Or maybe this is what you always look like when you're running Amman–Baghdad return routes every day. All you can do is hope for the best, maintain situational awareness and prepare (mentally) for the worst.

As a rule, I think it's really important to talk to pilots and express gratitude for their skills, which is exactly what I did. "Hey mate, thanks for that," I said. "Oh shit," he shot back with a very broad Australian accent, which particularly stands out on a tarmac in the Middle East. "You're an Aussie! Sorry about that dive, but I was pretty keen on dodging a group of local militia stationed just over the rise there on the edge of the runway, waiting to have a go. A rocket propelled grenade launcher up the ass doesn't make for a proper landing."

"Um, nice work," I said, smiling back at him. I kept my "Oh my Gods" to myself as I stepped down the rusted steps, which I was pretty certain had been dragged across the desert during the first Gulf War in the early 1990s.

Welcome to the war zone

I kept calm and carried on as I walked towards the customs hall. I was hoping it was air-conditioned as the sweat began to instantly express out of my forehead. When I opened the door, I walked into what I could only compare to a giant, rundown hot yoga studio.

I immediately scanned the scene and realised I was the only female in the sparsely populated room. You can imagine how nervous this made me feel, so I pretended to be reading my briefing folder as I walked, trying to look very busy, very focused – not a target for kidnapping at all.

I've been told throughout my life that I have a severe and somewhat intimidating 'resting bitch face', so I fully engaged it as a defence tactic. "No one was going to mess with me in this customs hall", I said quietly to myself.

I silently handed my passport to the customs officer and hoped he didn't expect me to speak Arabic. I was super-fluent in one statement only: "Hi there, please don't shoot me".

My instructions were to look for the five security guards who would escort me to the compound. Looking across the room, I saw a team of former UK Special Forces guys draped with AK-47s, grenades and handguns. Scooping up my bag, I couldn't help but notice they were the best-looking group of men I had seen in a while. I can't lie. "This trip just got exponentially better," I remember thinking to myself, any thoughts to distract me from my new reality were welcome.

They were not, however, in the mood for any light-hearted banter or jokes from a young, single Aussie aid worker. Their job was to keep me alive, after all. As a result, they swiftly escorted me through the airport, across a road and into an underground parking garage. On our way there, it was impossible to ignore the bullet holes in every wall. Every single wall was clearly target practice.

Security detail

After an abbreviated security briefing in the searing heat of the underground garage, I was handed a helmet, flak jacket and a burqa. A burqa? What exactly did they expect me to do with this? Noticing the quizzical look which overtook my face, the tallest of the team leaned forward to inform me that I needed to wear it if I wanted to avoid being kidnapped and held for ransom. "You wouldn't last 30 seconds on the street," he said.

"Really?", I thought to myself. The gravity of the situation just got a whole lot clearer.

As for being ambushed while stopped in traffic, the game plan was made clear: "Don't move, if we get boxed in by militia, stay where you are – we'll handle it". My 'outside' voice could not help itself, muttering: "You bet you'll handle it, I'm the only one standing around this entire war zone without a loaded AK-47, four grenades strapped to my chest and a back-up semi-automatic Glock," (I leaned forward and pitched my vocals up here), "which I have used before at an unidentified underground shooting range in Israel, but I won't bore you with that right now. So yeah, boys, you'll handle it, I'll just sit in the back of the car while we're under fire."

I slowly crossed my arms for effect, highly animated rant over. They all looked at me. I expected some snappy comeback, but I got nothing. These guys were pros. All I got was poker faces. They were obviously trained to ignore highly strung mouthy females, as well as both Shia and Sunni militia. "I'm just saying, if someone wants to give me a gun, I'm cool with that. I do guns," I declared. Silence. Precisely no arms were forthcoming. But a very strong Irish accent suggested: "OK, I think we've covered everything here, let's move out." "Yes, exactly, let's move out," I mumbled as I nodded. I reminded myself that this was a war zone. Burqa on head – check. Working for an international aid group – check.

Arrived safely in Iraq – check. It was time I got myself on task.

Home from home

I sat silently in the back right-hand side of the armoured 1985 500 SE Mercedes as we navigated the road between the airport and the compound. We were in the middle of a five-car convoy, with two vehicles ahead of us and two behind. The cars in front were the advance team. The reason for them was if there was a roadside bomb, they'd connect with it first. The team behind us would come to the rescue. This was the theory, mind you. When does anything ever go as planned in a war zone?

We were travelling at warp speed and must have clocked 150 mph as we raced past the blown-up, blown-out wrecks of cars, trucks and other disfigured objects. Then a 10-car convoy, with lights and sirens, whizzed by us. They were slippery clean, jet black Chevys. "Let me guess, they're State Department?", I piped up, sarcasm in full flow. "They like to keep a low profile," said one of the guys. Everyone roared with laughter.

When we arrived at the compound, I was quickly shown to my room by a six-foot-five Chief of Security. Someone told me he was former MI5 – I had no reason to think otherwise. He was a serious operator. He told me how we would escape if the compound was overrun. "You need to get to the roof in less than 20 seconds, otherwise you'll be locked down here." He then swung open the kind of steel door there would have been on the Titanic, the sort that stopped megaton water breaches. "This is the door that you want to be on the right side of, if you hear the alarm, OK?" "Yes, that's all very OK," I thought.

"And not that it matters, but there's no hot water here," he added as a casual footnote. Rewind. Can we stay on this subject for another minute? "Like, you mean no hot water, ever? Not just between certain hours?", I asked. "Not any hours. And the shower heads are broken, so you have to use a bucket," he said. Since we were in a war zone and all, I let it go. As a general policy, I don't start pointless arguments with people who can kill me with their bare hands, because it's not like I just checked in at the Ritz-Carlton. "This is a war zone, Andrea," I reminded myself, "so adjust accordingly."

Living under stress

My objective in the following few weeks was to interview local Iraqis who had returned to restart their businesses after being given micro-finance grants from USAID (the United States Agency for International Development). These stories would form a business case for the same aid programs being extended.

This was a deeply insightful and rewarding project and it left me with three key lessons for effective teamwork in a chaotic and high-pressure environment. They became the same lessons that are directly transferable to any workplace and which I still teach to this day:

1. Get clear on the team's objectives.

2. Get comfortable with courteous confrontation.

3. Give everyone the chance to have a voice; the person who's manning the front gate might see something that saves a life, in this case.

There's no need to set an alarm in Baghdad's 'Red Zone'. Tragically, every day, workday or otherwise, began the exact same way – being awakened to the sounds of car bombings in the morning markets. The gunfire was constant and happening just over the wall of the compound in which I was stationed. Bizarrely, you got used to the gunfire. After about an hour, it was just background noise, like a lawnmower running up and down your neighbour's lawn. You just learnt to ignore it, because it was part of the environment.

On a less violent and more personal note, I was distressed by the number of starving and stray kittens I would see in the area. They would sometimes be separated from their mothers and would cry out for them. Even amidst the chaos, I found it heartbreaking.

The level of distraction was off the charts, so every day it was critical to simplify our objectives and stay on point. Every morning, my team and I ran through the checklist to keep us laser-focused and on task. It's a habit I maintain to this day.

Having a master list beside me all day, shortlisting tasks and hustling through to strike them off by 6pm is how I work. I don't finish my work day until my list of tasks has been zeroed out. When you're clear of distractions and absolute about your objectives, there's no downward drag in the days that follow.

Life inside the aid workers' barracks was simple; sleep as much as you could and always next to a helmet and a torch. If the compound was somehow overrun, we could then find our way to the roof for extraction by the military. The reason for constant readiness was the militia launching rockets from behind the fence of the compound. Then there were the US helicopters on night patrols, sweeping across the roof every 20 minutes. The building would shake as they passed, so sleep patterns were easily broken.

All of this only added to a seriously tense environment. Sensing this, my camera crew and I agreed that if something bothered us, we'd put it on the table right away. The policy proved effective in reducing tension and increasing efficiency. Courteous confrontation builds trust and confidence and keeps everyone playing the 'outside game' instead of wasting time on any form of internal politics or unnecessary drama that might follow. No matter how intense an environment gets, never allow drama to undermine the spirit and cohesiveness of the team. If it does, there will always be a cost. That was something we could not afford.

Bribes and losses

During my time in Baghdad, I made a point of walking around the compound for meet-and-greets with the people in charge of the non-profit agency. On one particular occasion, I swung around the corner of a room in one of the buildings and saw a team of people scurrying about. Lined up along the left-hand wall of a large room was cash in the form of US dollars. Endless rows of greenbacks were piled from floor to ceiling.

I had an idea of what a bank vault might look like, but this was different. It was a startling sight. I had never seen so much money at one time in my entire life. There was easily US$5m in my direct line of sight; probably more like US$10m. Think about that for a moment: 10 million US dollars in cash. One of the staff members would later tell me that everyone there was paid in cash. "No doubt," I replied. "It's apparently everywhere." Sure, I got that we were in a violent, active war zone, but the payroll arrangement did strike me as a little, well... loose. There were stacks and stacks of cash bound together with rubber bands. From what I could tell, there wasn't any form of checks and balances, either, no cash-police and no extra security. Nothing? That's quite a policy.

I was told that all bribes or losses were built into our budget. 'Losses' was a very loose term for theft. I was new to the non-profit world and the way they did business, so I held my tongue. However, I did find it a bit alarming.

I heard rumours about the annual staff retreat that was coming up. It was a huge financial spend that was held at a five-star resort in the state of Pennsylvania. When I asked my boss about it, I discovered that not only were we expected to spend three full days with our colleagues playing stupid team-building games, we were also going to be given iPods and other extravagant gifts. Worst of all, it was compulsory – there was no way to 'opt out' of the trip. I estimated the cost of sending 300 people to the resort to be around half a million US dollars. As it turns out, I underestimated by a long shot.

The entire experience with the non-profit and how they did business sent up red flags across the board. It wasn't just the retreat, which was an obvious misspend, it was everything. The cost to move about in Baghdad was, at minimum, US$5,000 or more. Five thousand US dollars for my team to take me to

Saddam's former palace – which had been taken over by the State Department (and set up as a massive ping-pong hall – no kidding). I had one meeting there and if I knew then how much it had cost, I would have picked up the phone and called someone instead. It was my most expensive ride on record, by a long way.

Let's not forget about the walls of cash and the lack of accounting. Every time I turned around, I saw inconsistencies and things that didn't stack up. I was already suffering from sleepless nights, and the added fear of being kidnapped, but this really got into my head. I wasn't a total idealist about the non-profit world, but I was on high alert for anything that could be fair game in the public's eye.

As the head of communication, it was my job to flag these types of concerns. Anything that could be a news story had to be raised with my boss. What I was witnessing was a laundry list of potentially career-ending headlines for the board and the CEO. I began writing an email to my boss, where I made it clear that waste, fraud or misappropriation of government funds would result in a reputational disaster for the company. It never occurred to me for a moment that I was looking at job suicide. I was literally typing up my own exit.

I had no idea what would happen next or how I would manage it, but it was nothing I would ever wish upon anyone who felt as though they were living out their dream job. It was the first in a series of lessons that I could ultimately use to help others recover from major career setbacks.

While the future of work looks different for all of us, the key survival skills are the same. In the following chapters I'll explain what these key skills are and how they'll help you develop a #FutureFIT approach. These are the skills that we're not formally taught in school, university or anywhere else along the education journey, bizarrely. These are the skills that land us the job, keep us in the game and help us build long-standing relationships that can swing open new doors as our careers progress. We need to invest equally in these 'soft' skills as we do in the hard ones, because we're entering a phase where the responsibility for finding, securing and delivering work is shifting to the individual in ways we have not seen before. And how we apply those skills will need to be different in each different environment.

Building reputation capital

*"In order to keep up with the world of 2050, you
will need not merely to invent new ideas and products
– you will above all need to reinvent yourself again
and again."* –YUVAL NOAH HARARI

We're heading into an environment where it will be more
important than ever before to have developed a personal brand
and 'reputation capital' in order to excel in the workforce. As
we move towards more flexible work arrangements where we
have less face-to-face contact with colleagues and looser contracts with our managers, our reputation and the trail it leaves
will be more relevant than ever. More hiring decisions will be
made on the move, and without us in the room.

There will be no difference between how a manager views a
major consumer brand and a personal brand. The same line of
inquiry will remain: can I trust them, are they offering a valuable product, do they have a strong point of difference, do they
have the ability to influence? As trust expert Rachel Botsman
explains, our values, intentions, behaviours and capabilities

will be profoundly important in a new world where reputation will be the measure of how much a community trusts you.

Our reputation will have a far greater real-world value across the marketplace. It will leave markers. Perhaps when we finish a project we'll be rated, just as we are as passengers in an Uber. And when we're face-to-face with clients, we'll need to:

- pitch our skill-set with clarity and ease
- communicate what we love doing; and
- articulate how we generate value for stakeholders.

These elements require precise definition and delivery. We can't expect a manager to have confidence in us if we don't have the confidence to know, and communicate, what differentiates us across our department, business and industry.

Back from Baghdad: a new kind of war zone

I had just sat down at my desk in Washington D.C., when my boss swung around the corner, gripping both sides of the door frame. He looked distraught, which was unusual for a man of his calibre and capacity to manage chaos. A great friend and mentor, my boss Rick Santos had personally pulled me out of the television game for my role in the not-for-profit.

"I'm heading to the CEO's office. He's letting go of a few people. And you're one of them. He wants you gone," he said with a drawn-out reluctance. "I'm giving you the heads-up, Andrea. This won't be official until tomorrow."

It was a stinging ambush, and a very personal one at that. Not only did the CEO not like me, he now knew I was across his misconduct. I was gutted, but somehow managed not to break down in front of Rick. I saved that for 30 minutes later when I walked through my front door. I cried the ugly cry into most of the night. I was devastated. I asked myself questions I knew I had no answers for. It was a bombshell. And the blast radius shot through every cell in me. But I literally gave myself no time to dwell on it.

The next morning, my alarm went off at 7am sharp. Still broken and processing the situation, I sat up. Souvenirs from a punishing five years on the road were everywhere... the pile of 'go-bags' waiting for my next assignment, my cat Maddie, rescued from a French restaurant, and a range of press credentials from over the years. These were time stamps of my life. And now I had to create a new one, ready or not.

No one was going to solve this for me. No one was going to rescue me. There was no emergency fund, and certainly no magic trust fund or family support to buffer me through such a bruising. Despite the setback and the deep well of vulnerability I was struggling in, I wasn't ready to pack up and return to Sydney. For the next two weeks, I made a deal with myself to sideline my emotions and go as hard as I could for every decent communications job on Capitol Hill.

By 8am I was on-task with a plan of career resurgence, or in this case, resurrection. It was time to hit the phones. I quickly shortlisted everyone I could think of who could help. This wasn't a list of people to console me or commiserate with me on losing my job, this was a list of real friends, of life-liners. They are the kind who would work the phones for me like a team of reporters on a fast-moving story – my very own 'board of directors'.

The first calls were to my nearest, and most reliable, tribe. They included Laura Capps, a former speechwriter for President Bill Clinton, who was a Senior Vice President at the Ocean Conservancy, and Melissa Wagoner, who was the Press Secretary in the Office of Senator Edward M. Kennedy on Capitol Hill. They knew my purpose as intimately as I did myself: *to connect with people and help them communicate with authority.* I was brutally candid with each of them. "I've been made redundant. I obviously need to find a job, but here's where it gets interesting – I have 10 days to do it. If I don't, I have to leave the country. I need your help."

We divvied up the contacts and hit the phones. Our mission was clear – to find out what projects were live, who was hiring and what jobs were already in process. Phone calls, text messages and a flood of email exchanges followed. It was like running a mini campaign with my own private SWAT team of recruiters. Every time I engaged with a lead or contact, I was completely transparent about the situation. Transparent, but not desperate.

Within a few days, I had tactfully joined a job application process that was well underway for a major advocacy movement whose purpose it was to 'Save Darfur' from genocide. The role reported directly to Jerry Fowler, a widely respected leader on human rights. Just nine days after losing my 'dream gig', I received a call midway through ordering a double shot espresso at Logan Circle Starbucks. Jerry offered me the job. I even had the courage to ask for an extra US$10,000 in salary, to which he agreed.

My morning coffee had never tasted so good, especially now that I could afford it. I was completely stoked. My board of directors had worked the phones, conveyed the situation and helped me land an amazing gig. It was my job to lead the communication campaign to end the genocide in Darfur. What a privilege. A disturbing conflict, but what a job, to try to bring peace to the region. It was a role sharply aligned with my capabilities and perfectly aligned with my purpose. The lesson with hindsight here is: my reputation capital had real world value in the market. There's no way I could have dropped into a candidate process so late in the game unless someone rated me.

Reputation capital and a purpose-led pivot

By now I trust the placement of this chapter has not been lost on you. Indeed, what could be more apt than opening a book on how to 'future-proof' ourselves for an era of unknowns, than sharing a chapter of my life that has been, by far, the most destabilising and yet defining?

My conditioning as a journalist had prepared me well – nothing is more stressful than the rush of breaking news. By stressful, I mean, if you don't embrace the pace of a rapidly developing story, then you find yourself irrelevant. If you miss a key development or take your eye off the game, you quickly find yourself sidelined by a Chief of Staff who'll no longer entrust you with the next big story. As a reporter, you prove your relevance every single day by getting the story right, and hopefully before your competitors. If you have a bad day, then half a million people witness it too. Such public accountability wasn't always a great feeling, but it was an exceptionally motivating one. With hindsight, in digging myself out of a career crisis, I had applied the same rules – embrace the pace of the chaos, and work the problem until you hit the deadline.

In the following years, I was able to recognise that the function of my role in Iraq was right for me. The culture of leadership, however, was completely wrong. I had found myself tangled in a regime operating in complete conflict with my life's learnings, values and beliefs – not just in a professional sense, but a personal one too. In fact, for all its hurt and havoc, this chapter had taught me more about myself than any before it. Confronted by people, systems and circumstances that were utterly *wrong for me*, I had cemented my understanding of what was *right*, or more specifically, what was *right for me*; the stuff I would never budge on, the stuff that could never be grey, what I stood for, the values that grounded and drove my decisions. It was an inside-out game. Once I got crystal clear on the inside, I was able to act with intention on the outside.

'Owning' my reputation capital and recognising that it has a real-world value has been one of the critical constants amid changing personal and professional winds in my life – and thus, a fundamental pillar of this book. So... what does it all mean, why does it matter and how can you sharpen your personal brand in the pursuit of career advancement?

Personal brand

Three years ago I direct-messaged Belinda Wall, Founding Director of Brand Amplified, to congratulate her on having the most original thoughts on Instagram. Having worked with some of Australia's fastest growing startups including 2XU, through to global consulting firms like PwC, it didn't take long before I pulled Belinda onto the CareerCEO crew.

According to Wall, personal brand is an umbrella construct for the many elements that combine to define precisely who we are. "Personal brand," says Wall, "is both simple and complex:

"Simple, because it is purely what makes us, us.

"Complex, because it encompasses *everything* that makes us, us.

"A personal brand is multi-dimensional – it's:

- the **physical person**
- their **digital footprint**
- their **values** system
- their **promises and actions** and, of course,
- the **perception** others have of them.

"Furthermore, your personal brand includes the
expectations others have of you, and your legacy."

Clearly, then, personal brand is far more than our résumé – or
in today's vernacular, far more than our LinkedIn profile. It
is not merely a laundry list of our professional capabilities or
accomplishments, nor a chronological summary of our careers.
"It's what we say we'll do, and what we do, combined. It's the
moods we set, our tone, style and how we make others feel when
they're with us. It's what people say about you when you're not
in the room," says Wall.

When I hear all this, or anything about personal brand,
one word comes to mind: reputation. If you were yet to com-
prehend the relevance of personal brand, I have no doubt it's
crystallising now. Because let's face it, who doesn't care about
their reputation? To this, I'll add an often confounding truth.
Your personal brand already exists. It's whether or not you're
actively controlling it, that is the question.

"*Managing* your personal brand simply means taking control of the essence of *you*," says Wall.

"Just as is the case for branding at large, being strategic
about your personal brand takes a consideration of
multiple touch points, and leveraging those touch points
to realise your particular goals and objectives. Once
considered and managed, the true value of personal brand
is realised. In this regard, personal brand is about owning,
articulating and showcasing your earned, true and unique
value proposition. It's also an opportunity to step beyond
career development mode, into career advancement."

Why it all matters

Brand, marketing and leadership gurus have long championed the value of defining and living by our 'why' or 'purpose'.

Acclaimed organisational consultant Simon Sinek has published on the power of starting with, and finding, our why – for brands, individuals and teams alike; that there's nothing more powerful or purposeful than communicating and living not by *what* we do or produce, but the reason *why* we do it all. Award-winning business author Seth Godin has flagged the benefits of adopting core brand marketing (purpose) principles to build trust and goodwill among those who can support your goals. Leading business and brand consultant James Kerr revealed the exceptional value of character, purpose, authenticity, discipline, and a fundamentally why-based values system, over talent, when it came to building the most successful sports team of all time, the New Zealand All Blacks. Research by Wharton management and psychology professor Adam Grant tells us that identifying our why is key to staying happy and productive on the job.

This is just a selection of highlights from an exhaustive bank of 'why' resources, advocates, authors, research papers and perspectives, but the takeaway is clear. Defining and living our why is not only valuable but proven, celebrated and showcased by successful people across the globe each and every day. And if you're still after a compelling ROI, how about personal fulfilment, engagement and positive energy? Psychologists have found that humans are more motivated by personally meaningful goals than by external rewards such as money or status. When we love what we do, it shows. We're lit up by our passion, we put in extra effort, we're a source of epic ideas and we signal real confidence.

It's uplifting, then, to learn that some of the world's largest organisations and organisational leaders – critical architects in our future of work – are now identifying the value of 'purpose' more than ever too. In a comprehensive global report on *Preparing for tomorrow's workforce, today,* PwC surveyed more than 1,200 business and HR leaders from 79 countries. The 2018 paper explores the myriad ways transformation is impacting workforces; how we work, the importance of work in our lives, and what we mean by work.

Among the findings is the following observation by Lynda Gratton, Professor of Management Practice at London Business School:

> "Despite the changing context of work, people's desire for 'good work' – defined as work with purpose in an environment that is nurturing – has remained remarkably consistent over the years. It is imperative for corporate leaders to embrace this concept and focus on crafting a great *people experience* in the context of, but not distracted by, wider trends such as technological development."

Spearheading the white paper's list of key priorities for action was "Creating a competitive advantage through a more engaging 'people experience'", coupled with a definition of 'people experience' itself, which read: "The environment at work that gives people their sense of purpose, including the way offices are organised, the arrangements for working hours, the commitment by leadership to a mission and the training and support offered by human resources."

Know thyself

Purpose is certainly creeping into the discourse of workforce transformation. In the context of preparing ourselves, as individuals, for the Fourth Industrial Revolution – an era of unprecedented transformation and change through to 2050 – one of the most compelling arguments for 'owning' our why has come from bestselling Israeli professor Yuval Noah Harari. In his latest book, *21 Lessons for the 21st Century*, Harari explores the exceptional developments technology is set to offer human-kind, while also raising a red flag to the dangers in store for those who operate without volition.

Harari maintains that technology isn't necessarily bad, but you need to know what you want it to help you with. If you are not clear on this then technology will decide for you. Technology is improving in the way it understands humans, so you need to make sure technology is serving you, not the other way round.

He says you only have to look outside at people wandering around with their gaze glued to their smartphones, oblivious of their surroundings. Who's in control there?

"...As biotechnology and machine learning improve, it will become easier to manipulate people's deepest emotions and desires, and it will become more dangerous than ever to just follow your heart. When Coca-Cola, Amazon, Baidu or the government knows how to pull the strings of your heart and press the buttons of your brain, could you still tell the difference between yourself and their marketing experts?"

Harari's advice therefore is to "know thyself". It's not an easy task to get to know yourself better, but it is essential in order to understand what you want from life.

This is powerful stuff – confronting, perhaps, but too incredible not to share. What attracts me most to Harari's observations, however, is his inherent ability to offer a positive – an *actionable* positive "know thyself". The projections might be frightening to some, but the opportunity is clear. We need to take control, to consider who we are, to know ourselves, to know what makes us unique, to know what we want from life, and to claim the driver's seat. Quite simply, if we're pursuing #FutureFITNESS we must 'own' our purpose in life, or else be 'owned'.

It's personal: agency is king

As we stare down a future of unmatched digitisation, automation, unimaginable technological innovation, and relentless transformation, could agency – our personal autonomy and initiative – be the next competitive advantage? I put the question to my resident branding brains-trust, and fellow Harari fan, Wall.

> "Absolutely. In today's connectivity-obsessed climate where things are noisier, more cluttered and changeable than ever, operating in the absence of a personal compass has never been riskier. When we're unsure, or haven't stopped to think about our 'why', we often invest disproportionately in our 'what' – our work – the 'rat race' and merely getting sh*t done. This can be problematic. When we're faced with copious, complex or challenging decisions, or made unexpectedly redundant, for instance, finding our way can be overwhelmingly difficult. Purpose is power. Purpose is efficient, consistent, intention-based behaviour. Operating *with* purpose – a powerful inner compass – could be tomorrow's greatest asset."

Your 4-point personal brand plan

Where to from here? The following four-point framework is designed to support your personal brand distillation and journey.

Consider > Create > Amplify > Engage

Consider kicks off with the absolute fundamentals; the non-negotiable foundations of a powerful personal brand – defining the essence of *you*. You'll also learn how to master the art of verbally communicating your brand in moments that matter.

For those keen and ready to level up even further, **Create**, **Amplify** and **Engage** step you through some key considerations for a personal brand strategy. Please note, however, that a proactive 'strategic push' to develop such a strategy may not always be right for, or required by, every individual. Ultimately, it will depend on your particular set of goals and desires at a particular point in time.

Make no mistake, there is huge value in mastering your Consider foundations alone. Once you've identified what drives, ignites, and separates you from the rest of the world, you'll have found your 'inner knowing' – your inner compass! This all takes serious focus, commitment and time, so please don't expect to nail it straight up. Work on it. Invite contribution and feedback from those you trust. Give it your all.

1. Consider

Know thyself

Before you can start to tell the story of 'you' and build your personal brand, you need to identify what your story is. What makes you different, relevant and valuable to your target audience? To reach your career and business goals, you need to understand your strengths, skills and passions, the values that separate you from your competitors and reinforce how you stand out. Be the investigator of your personal brand. Do your research on 'you' to understand what makes you unique and different from everyone else.

Take time to work through these key thoughts:

- What am I obsessed with? Who am I? Who am I not?
- What is valuable to me?
- What tasks make me feel the happiest?
- What makes me stand out?
- Why do people come to me?
- When was the last time I felt real meaning in my work – what was I doing?
- What are my key strengths?

These can be challenging questions, so here's a scenario to offer some extra perspective:

This morning, your boss taps you on the shoulder and asks for a quick chat. "I've got some unfortunate news," says Boss X. "I've just been informed of a major restructure across the business, which means I need to cut our team in half, almost immediately. I'm seeing the CEO in 15 minutes, and need to communicate why you should stay. What do you want me to say?"

How does this situation make you feel? How well could you communicate your worth, in a concise yet compelling manner, particularly when under pressure? How do you want that conversation to sound?

While your instinct might lead you to a response peppered with adjectives like *trustworthy, dedicated, honest, hardworking, reliable* and *punctual*, such qualities fail to separate you from your competitors, and sure as hell won't impress the CEO. Furthermore, generic 'assets' like these are a given for anyone operating in today's professional arena. Can you build on the generic words that might come to mind first?

As you tackle the aforementioned brainstorm on 'you', challenge yourself to come up with a takeaway of three to five sentences to describe what makes you unique and valuable. If full sentences are a challenge, feel free to start with a single word that speaks to your differentiation. Some great examples include:

- I'm a curious thinker who loves nothing more than a new challenge or problem to solve.
- Strategic, yet also tactical, I flex easily between big picture projects and execution.
- Forensic with the detail, I'm a financial analyst who finds the mistakes that others miss.
- I was the self-confessed 'maths geek' at school. Now I'm a career CFO.
- Trusted by peers and leaders alike, I'm a respected project manager with the ability to engage stakeholders on all levels.
- The 'notorious nurturer', I'm the glue that cares for the team. From birthdays to BBQs, I'm the energetic optimist who celebrates the stuff that matters.

If your three to five sentences make you stand out and are of benefit to a potential employer, collaborator or stakeholder, you're on the money.

Personal branding is powerful because it sends a clear, consistent message about who you are and what you have to offer. A strong, authentic personal brand helps you become known for what you're good at, sets you apart from everyone else, and can position you as a valued and trusted specialist in your field. It's now time to develop your personal value pitch.

Communicate your value

Often termed an elevator pitch, a personal value pitch is a short summary used to quickly and simply communicate who you are, and the value this holds. 'Elevator pitch' harks back to the idea that it should be possible to deliver the pitch in the time (30 seconds to two minutes) of an elevator ride (co-occupied by a 'person of note'). Some prefer to think of it as a BBQ pitch, when they're introduced to a mate's mate (who happens to own a successful startup with attractive career opportunities). Whatever the case, your challenge is to drive a conversation that's interesting and valuable enough to warrant ongoing banter, or the exchange of details for future exploration. Sounds simple, but communicating our value in a way that doesn't make us sound like a show-off (or leave the other party yawning), takes practice, practice, practice.

Building on this step, your next task is to extend your differentiated qualities into a set of tidy talking points. Here are some openers to get you started:

- My job (intention/purpose of your role)[1] is ...
- Colleagues would say ...
- The highlight of my career so far is ...
- I love what I do because ...
- One of my most rewarding projects has been ...

An important addition to consider building into your 'job descriptor' is a metric. Metrics give us currency and credibility. For example, *"My job is Managing Director of CareerCEO"* versus *"My job is to train 900 people a year to communicate with authority"*. The first version doesn't mean much, so I can't expect it to resonate with people in moments that matter. The second option, however, not only paints a clear picture of what I do, but packs some punch in terms of the scale and scope of my work. Candid, credible and conversational – tick.

---

1   In terms of describing what you do for a living, be sure to avoid referencing your actual job title, which typically means nothing to the rest of the world. Instead, consider the purpose of what you do – the actual function of your role. Use plain and simple (BBQ friendly) English, and avoid jargon. What does Wall say when I ask what she does for a living? "I work with people and brands to distil their value and communicate it to key audiences in creative, engaging ways." Not a Brand Marketing Consultant in sight.

I often hear people say, "But I don't want to PR myself." I get it. Work is not a public relations campaign. No one wants to be 'that person' artificially promoting their way to the top. But why should we expect the CEO to 'buy into us', if we're uncomfortable owning and articulating our value ourselves? Your pitch is about connecting. It's about offering something of interest, instead of regurgitating the title on your business card. Not only is referencing your official title out of date, it's dull and diminishes the true value you bring to the world.

Importantly, your 'tidy talking points' must feel natural to you, and this will of course flex with the audience and context at hand (i.e. you might want to share some impressive recent project metrics and a little corporate jargon with the CEO in the elevator, but adopt a more informal approach with your BBQ mate). The point is to develop a folio of options to select from when a 'free kick' next lands in your corner.

Audience and resources

As demonstrated above, when considering and defining your personal brand you need to be clear on who your audience is and the best way to get through to them. Think carefully about the following elements:

- **Audience:** Who do I need to influence, why should they care about me, and what value can I offer them?
- **Execution:** What tools, platforms and channels should I use to reach and engage my audience?
- **Advisors:** Do I have a highly trusted 'board of directors' at the ready? Who can I turn to for candid advice when I need it most? Who will hold me to account, and call me out when I'm off-purpose or off-brand? Do I have diversity in expertise, experience and opinion on my personal board? What's in it for them?

2. Create

Platforms

Determine the platforms you need to be on, and the role they're going to play for your personal brand either personally or professionally (i.e. some platforms might be strictly personal or 'passion-project' based, while others remain professional). Tweak privacy settings accordingly. Noting the semantics of both your industry and professional goals, are existing platforms OK (LinkedIn, Facebook, Medium, Instagram, relevant industry websites or networks), or do you need to create something bespoke – a website or blog perhaps – to convey your character and point of difference to its fullest?

Content and assets

Ask yourself:

- Will my content and assets be visual, verbal or both?
- Will I simply be sharing, liking and engaging with existing content, or publishing entirely new perspectives of my own?
- Will my strategy be fundamentally online, or require in-person engagements too?
- What is the intention behind my content?

3. Amplify

Thinking about the platforms you're on, the groups and events you're involved with, the audiences you're targeting, how much time you have and how much time they have, ask yourself:

- What's the best way to broadcast my messages so they're likely to cut through?
- When and how often will I share a perspective/piece of content?
- Will I speak or get involved in special industry events?

- Could I take my expertise to organisations outside of my immediate professional circle?

4. Engage

Finally: never point, shoot and assume it's going to work. Understand that strategic personal branding always involves a two-way 'value' exchange that needs to be watched, tweaked and refined along the way. Like the savviest of brand managers, you must be both your greatest fan and your harshest critic.

At regular intervals, measure and check the effectiveness (engagement) of your strategy. Ask yourself:

- Am I cutting through/getting noticed?
- Are people valuing my perspective/contribution?
- Is it different and compelling?
- Am I doing anything to support others/'pay it forward' along the way?
- Are people engaging with my desired call-to-action?

Or is it time to rebrand? A strong personal brand should be constantly evolving.

At some point in time, we might want to take on a new challenge, start a business or shift into more meaningful work. Sometimes the changes are major – a massage therapist becomes a life coach or a lawyer starts up an IT business. Sometimes the shift is far more subtle, like an executive who wants to advance but needs to overcome a reputation that he's 'not good with numbers'. Your pivot might make perfect sense to you, but more often than not, a considered 'rebrand' is likely required. This will mean retracing your Consider > Create > Amplify > Engage steps and, ultimately, persuading others to embrace your new brand and take you seriously with a fresh set of brand promises, actions and proof points to match.

* * *

In closing this personal brand discussion, let me leave you with a thought from one of the world's foremost behavioural scientists, Brené Brown: "We're not curious about things that we don't know a little bit about. We have to know a little bit about something to be curious about it."

Curiosity is an emotion. Every decision is affected on some level by emotions and, as we know, emotions are powerful. You can drive more conversions, more conversations, more opportunities, more exchanges, more collaborations and innovations by drawing out an individual's curiosity. So let's get people curious about us. Let's get proactive about our personal brand. Let's build our reputation capital.

Aftermath of the non-profit fraud

As a footnote to the chapter and my story of abruptly being made redundant... the memo I sent to my boss was referenced on the front page of *The Washington Post*.

It was part of a comprehensive investigation that detailed how the co-founder and head of a non-profit company was accused of misappropriation of government funds. He was ultimately found not to be operating outside of the rules, however the entire board was fired, USAID suspended funding and the business had to change its name to survive. The founder had to pay back US$2m that he had previously paid to himself and his wife in the form of bonuses.

The story played out precisely how I said it would in my email – the organisation would face a reputational crisis which would effectively shut it down. The aid group was delivering incredible programs around the world that were relieving the suffering of so many people. And so many staff of the organisation were putting themselves in very hostile situations to make this happen, including myself and my treasured colleague James Stephenson, who has since passed away. This entire story was a devastating development for all involved.

3

Sharpening communication skills

"Communication is about impact, not output"
—TIM WARD, CO-AUTHOR OF *THE MASTER COMMUNICATOR'S HANDBOOK*

We'll need to be 'super-communicators' by 2025. Superior communication skills will be necessary for us to excel in the future of work as individuals, as teams and as leaders.

As individuals, our work will be increasingly dependent on others in an environment marked by rapid flows of information and high levels of uncertainty. We'll need to manage complex scenarios, dynamic processes and the interplay of our work with the goals and processes of others. We'll also need to collaborate with others to discover, design, deliver or deploy our solutions.

Clear communication skills are an extension of thinking clearly. To accelerate our careers, we'll all need to be efficient thinkers who can review, distil and disseminate critical bodies of information in faster, more impactful ways than ever before. The ability to pitch ideas, concepts and strategies to business leaders requiring our advice on how to navigate disruptions on the horizon, will also be part of our capability portfolio. Talking in parallel to running a 40-page slide deck is over.

To be effective leaders, we must be original, bolder and boast the ability to capture and engage our audience through clear, masterful communication. Clear communication skills will also open doors for the jobs we want and deserve. People managers, including most recently one from Atlassian, continue to tell me that candidates with strong communication skills win over technical capability every time.

Motivation nation: breaking news

There is no sharper example of how to interpret information at breakneck pace, narrow it and communicate it with impact, than every single day I was assigned a story to file for the 6pm news.

Every day of my television reporting career, I had to become an expert in a new topic, emerging trend or breaking tragedy. Some days, I had eight full hours to interpret a medical research report on a new malaria vaccine, but other days I had less than eight minutes between arriving at an asylum seeker protest and going live as the lead story. In every case, my job was to speak with authority in a clear and compelling way, leaving the audience informed, and confident of the facts.

Every technique used by broadcast news reporters applies directly to the workplace, where the objective is the same: to capture and influence our audience with command and credibility. Foundational to our #FutureFIT game plan, I'll kick off by sharing one of my most vivid 'breaking news' memories.

36 missed calls

I was at least 20 minutes into a conversation about campaign tactics with a Capitol Hill staffer when I reached into my handbag to casually check my phone. It was the first time I had eaten lunch outside the office in my entire career and up until that very second, I thought it suited me. *Bistrot du Coin* was a French restaurant on Connecticut Ave NW, Washington D.C.; a place known for its buzz and buckets of mussels. I wasn't interested in either, I was only there for the steak frites and superb French accents.

I took a lightning glance at my screen. Under the date of April 16, 2007, it read: 36 missed calls. THIRTY-SIX MISSED CALLS. The buzz of the lunchtime crowd flatlined. WOW. Someone was dead. Or it was 9/11 all over again. Whatever the story, it was breaking and it was big time.

I was overcome with a wave of anxiety as I stumbled to return the most recent call – it was the Seven News bureau in Los Angeles. Mike Amor told me, "There's a big story breaking." There had been another mass shooting, this time across the Virginia Tech campus in Blacksburg. "At least 30 dead. Get a camera and get on the road," he instructed me. "I'll get the first flight I can, but you need to file for 6pm – Sydney will want you live off the top. Get your ass there, mate. Massive story, mate."

Evacuating the restaurant in a personal best, I hailed the first cab on the corner. I screamed, "1300 N St," to the driver and started thinking through what was missing from my 'go-bag' (the ready-packed rucksack with a week's supply of clothes, allowing me to exit the apartment onto a news story in 60 seconds or less).

First priority: hire a cameraman. Even though the story was only 20 minutes old, I knew every freelancer would already be assigned. Depending on who was available, the next few days would either be really arduous or really effortless. I called the Reuters desk where I was a regular and asked who was free. It was Rohan – an incredibly tall, very loud Scotsman who we all suspected was not just any run of the mill alcoholic, but a highly functioning one. It made me nervous. I shook my head. Sobriety was critical for this particular story.

I secured him, held the cab while I summonsed my go-bag, and screamed over to Capitol Hill. As my cab pulled up, Rohan slammed shut the trunk of his car and turned around. He picked up camera gear in both hands and, with a cigarette hanging out of the side of his mouth, declared, "When will these Yanks learn, not everyone needs a farkin' gun!"

Rohan had what I considered a vintage Land Rover, not exactly a news car, but as long as we got there by the 6pm Sydney news slot, I couldn't care less. My phone rang repeatedly as the Seven News foreign editor updated me with instructions about the live truck he was booking, requests for live crosses for each state bulletin, and the developing news he was seeing on CNN. We hit the road and, as I finally caught my breath, I took a minute to cancel every commitment I had for the coming days.

It was a four-hour drive to the Virginia Tech campus, which I assumed meant five hours in this car – and I was just about right. I spent every moment scrambling for information. In 2007, the Blackberry was very much on trend, and it was all I had: no iPad, no Mac with wireless device. Compared to today's news tools, using a Blackberry was much like using a teaspoon to empty a bath. But a 'teaspoon' was all I had, so I cracked on and did the best I could.

It was hours since the '36 missed calls' moment. We hadn't even hit the location and I was already exhausted. I'm sure there's a medical term for it, but the adrenalin that surges through your body on days like this is extreme, which explains why every reporter I know can virtually nap on cue. It was about 7pm (Virginia time) when we passed the town sign.

The plan for this one was clear: grab three or four interviews, feed them back to Sydney then stay on campus until going live at 6pm Sydney time, which was another few hours away at 2am local time – not when I am known to produce my best work, by any means. The plan always appears relatively straightforward.

The car had not come to a complete stop when I opened the door and literally bailed up the first few people I could. Scanning the campus, it was like a scene from a movie. There were people wandering around, dazed and confused, hugging one another. The cold, harsh reality is that as a reporter, showing up to any tragedy means automatically compartmentalising any emotional response you may have to the scene. When you only have six minutes to gather interviews, you jettison the ability to care about what has actually taken place. Instead, you park those emotions for when you have time to deal with them.

On this particular night, I was so caught up with meeting the deadline that I utterly failed to recognise that some of my interviewees were in a state of medical shock. I also, embarrassingly, wasn't able to properly connect with the trauma of the victims, their families and the communities involved. So many lives were devastated in those few moments before the gunman took his own life.

This particular night was the beginning of a realisation that, for me, this reporting game was over. Landing in a local war zone, exploiting the pain of the people in a way that seemed voyeuristic and potentially opportunistic, then catching the first flight home, was not right. Nothing about it felt good. It lacked integrity. The rules of the game never allowed you the time to care. Maybe I was at my personal deadline.

In those few minutes though, it was game on: yell instructions at Rohan, fire brutally direct questions at survivors, then bark orders at the team in the satellite trucks who were feeding the material back to the network for the afternoon bulletin. Then, regroup for a series of live crosses into the main evening bulletin. At the time, this was the worst shooting massacre in US modern history.

You're the voice – you really are

I had never in my career been more nervous. This was a major breaking story and I was crossing to an icon of Australian television news, Ian Ross, who I grew up watching every morning on the *Today* show. I engaged the Navy SEAL box-breathing technique I mentioned in the first chapter at least five times. Breathe in for four seconds, hold for four and exhale for four. This slowed my heart rate down while I recited the opening to the story.

Unusually high winds had kicked up that night. In fact, it was so windy that some flights were diverted. The gusts were blowing over the lights anchored by sandbags. It was a biting cold five degrees Celsius. As far as set-ups go for a live cross, this one was a shocker. The wind, the lights and the uneasiness of everyone around me was nauseating. In addition, of course, 33 people had just been shot 100 metres away only hours before. There was genuine panic about this one, we were only 60 seconds from going to air and I still didn't know if the interviews had been cut in time for me to use them.

Rohan was talking to me while someone else fixed my microphone. "Can I run this down the back of your shirt?" He was kind enough to ask. "Go, go, go!", I quipped. As a reporter, it was standard operating procedure to have a cameraman or soundman run a mic cord down your shirt, or up your dress, and then tape it so it was hidden. There was rarely a time when I would notice it happening. The red light was on, and I was about to go live to the nation.

What I knew for sure as a broadcast news reporter was that our voice is the most powerful instrument we have to capture and hold an audience. Research by MIT says that our voice accounts for 40% of our impact, and that when it comes to outcomes of a conversation, body language accounts for a whopping 50%. Our voice is a tool to connect with those listening. Whether you're a news reporter going live to air, or a manager trying to sell a new idea to your team, having 'presence' and commanding the room requires an acute understanding of how we communicate. When we master our voice, our body language, our use of language, and have a clear framework to think on our feet, we communicate with credibility.

Vocal patterns

Our vocal patterns send strong signals, so let's be clear on the power of each element: the pitch, pace, tone and volume of our voice.

Pitch

Delivering a clear, concise line means speaking in our 'lower conversational pitch,' the same pitch we use in everyday discussions. Our breath comes from the belly, the powerhouse. When we have an audience we of course need to project, but sometimes we also have a microphone for this.

We desperately need to avoid pitching 'up' – when our inflection rises at the end of a sentence, we send signals of being in doubt about our content when, in fact, we're likely to be the expert in our field. Alongside this is 'vocal fry', a prevalent vocal tendency among young American women whereby they default to the lowest pitch they can produce. According to a 2014 US study by Duke University, the use of 'vocal fry' by younger women is severely damaging to the way they're perceived. Women who demonstrate this vocal pitch are perceived as less competent, less educated, less trustworthy and less hireable.

Thus, a few solid reasons to cut it out! (Note: most exchanges on any episode of *Keeping up with the Kardashians* offer a compelling case in point.)

Pace

When we use pauses and control our pace, we signal being in command. A comfortable and clear pace is what we are aiming for. An ideal speaking rate will allow you to comfortably increase your pace to create a sense of excitement, or slow your pace to emphasise the seriousness of a topic. If anything, the vast majority of us require slowing down by 10% to 20%. A shift as simple as this will enable us to have far more control, and signal greater command.

Tone

Our tone conveys our true feelings about the situation. In the workplace, striking a balance between warmth and authority is where we want to be. This equals credibility.

Volume

Read the room. Project if you need to. Be mindful that your message will likely get lost on those at the other end of the room if you're not speaking loudly enough. Ask for a microphone if you need to. Many women speak more softly by nature without even knowing it. Don't undermine your presence and purpose in a room by literally failing to be heard.

Your voice is the future

If you don't like the sound of your voice, I politely suggest that you find a way to get over it because there are very few people that do. Record yourself. Listen to yourself. Get to know your voice every day, because it's going to get a whole lot more relevant in ways that might surprise you.

Some business leaders believe 'voice' is the future for both individuals and businesses. A growing number of employers are even speeding up the hiring process by using voicemail to screen initial interviews. Candidates answer standard questions, and those who pass the initial verbal test move forward in the queue. US insurance giant Allstate is one such company. Forget about a warm smile to smooth over an awkward initial interview – we're now going to be judged in a soundbite.

Voice has been a core focus for Gary Vaynerchuk, Chairman of VaynerX and CEO of VaynerMedia, for the past two years. "Podcasting and the rise of Alexa voice is here today. Brands and individuals alike have gotten serious about audio. The problem is, there still isn't a lot of great original content to consume, which leaves a massive opportunity for those who can produce on another level. Think of it like Netflix, the companies that create the best originals are going to win. There is no doubt in my mind that the level of creative we are about to see from long-form audio-only 'sitcoms' is going to blow your mind," says Vaynerchuk.

Audio streaming in particular is up 76% year on year, eclipsing video with 250 billion annual streams. To this, Vaynerchuk adds, "I think this is just the beginning. Alexa and Google Home are another exciting space. More so than podcasting itself, I think Alexa is an incredible opportunity to win. If you consider podcasting to be the current go-to destination for creative, then Alexa skills are the beachfront property vacation, yet to be discovered and booked up by the masses."

For individuals like you and me, what opportunity does this staggering data (repeat: audio streaming up 76% year on year) offer us, and the businesses we run? Surely audio has to be one of the fastest, and cheapest, ways to connect with our community of stakeholders and bring them closer. When I run workshops in businesses across Australia, I often wonder how many (particularly of those comprising 40,000+ incredibly talented humans with exceptional stories) have created internal podcasts that could spin off into far greater external projects.

If you follow Vaynerchuk's work, you'll know his opinions are strong. I truly believe his forecasts on audio and voice have nailed where we need to be. "It's by far the most natural interface for humans to interact. We like to speak and listen. There was roughly 1.5X more audio consumed than video according to Nielsen statistics on streaming in 2016. This is HUGE. If your medium is voice, now is your time. Start creating today. Start a podcast, record your phone conversations with friends or call your relatives and host a talk-show. Develop an Alexa skill or start experimenting with Google Home. Before AR and VR and AI, audio is going to be the next major platform shift for consumer attention," he says.

Texting: out; voice memo: in

If creating a podcast isn't aligned with your career plan, then there's another way to get familiar with your tone – the voice memo. A voice memo is a simple short audio recording that lies in between a WhatsApp text chat and any number of instant messenger channels. No longer the exclusive domain of high-flying CEOs communicating with EAs, it's now a trend being adopted by savvy younger generations to connect with friends. And it's exploding – more than 200 million voice messages are being sent every day via WhatsApp alone. Once you start, you won't stop, because studies show that hearing someone's voice helps us build empathy just as effectively as if we were seeing their face.

For those who like the sound of this modern mode of messaging, it just gets better: another study shows that our sense of hearing may be even stronger than our sight when it comes to detecting emotion. Without visual cues of emotion to read from, the brain works overtime to pick up nuances in someone's voice. That's far more human than texting, where the subtext is so easily and routinely misinterpreted. Voice memos are today's walkie-talkie. And let's be honest, who didn't love using those? Roger that.

Body language: move like you mean it

Whether we like it or not, people make sweeping judgments about us based on the way we communicate with our body. When we understand the powerful role body language can play, walking into a room and delivering with 'presence' is easy.

Head tilt

The most common mistake we make is unconsciously tilting our head to one side when speaking with audiences that matter. For the receiver, this signals the presenter being in doubt.

Ground yourself

If you're standing up, plant your feet under your hips and establish a solid grounding. This will enable you to stabilise, to feel strong, to breathe deeply into your belly and take control.

No fidgeting

Don't unconsciously play with a pen or brush your hair off your face. Be mindful of the subtle habits you may have developed – the habits that particularly come into play when you're nervous. You may not be aware of small things that distract the audience from listening to your well-crafted content, so once again, be bold enough to video record yourself on your phone and practise, practise, practise.

Direct eye contact

Any presentation or meeting is foremost a conversation. It's about connecting with the audience, which is impossible if we're not making eye contact with people around us. Regardless of how nervous you may be, avoid scanning rapidly around the room. Don't miss the chance to be truly engaged and present in the moment.

Every word matters: language at work

On a weekly basis I'm asked, "How can I be taken more seriously at work?" Rarely is the roadblock to executive presence related to competency. Overwhelmingly, it resides in a lack of confidence to speak with authority.

Our use of language is a critical part of this equation. When it comes to the words we use at work, it's about impact, not about output. Whether we're around a boardroom table or running a meeting with our team, the purpose of our communication is not to 'talk out loud' and explore wildly irrelevant tangents while (attempting) to hold an audience captive. The purpose is to influence, inform and, in some cases, to get our ball over the line.

These are the moments when we are seen and heard in sound bites, in snappy short windows – and this is precisely where many of us miss the breakthrough window to build credibility. We unconsciously undermine our authority by using any combination of the four language patterns described below that downplay our capabilities and sideline our smarts.

"Sorry"

Avoid apologetic statements. Never open a meeting with, "I'm sorry, this won't take up much of your time," or "Sorry – can you all hear me?" Before you even get into your content, you're apologising for simply being there. You may not even recognise this as a habit, but it undermines your authority and leaves the audience questioning your ability.

"Just"

"Just" falls neatly into the category of tentative statements. "I'm just here to talk about the results." "Just a quick email about the project..." "Can I just add..." It can be a powerful adjective (a just request, he got his just desserts), but when you use 'just' to preface any running commentary, it becomes merely a light little filler that softens the seriousness of anything that follows. A high ranking female executive recently told me she reads her emails twice before sending them on, quite simply to ensure she hasn't included 'just' in her copy. It's an easy discipline we can all adopt!

"I'm not the expert"

Have you ever used these expressions in a meeting? "I'm not the expert on this." "I'm sure you might disagree..." "Just a random idea, but..." If you're cautious or hesitant about your content, there are alternative phrases to use that won't leave the audience wondering about your capability. Try "I'd like to propose this concept..." "The data indicates the following..." "Here's an idea to add to the mix."

"It's only my opinion"

This is the realm of a self-diminishing qualifier: "It's only my opinion." It's one of the lines that frustrates me the most because leading executives continue to tell me their staff are "paid to have an opinion – and if they don't have an opinion, then they probably shouldn't be on the team."

Own your opinion, declare it, and back it up with the evidence. Get familiar with more confident, impressive expressions that serve to build trust with your audience. "The team's view on this project..." "The collective view of the department..." "My take on the situation is..." Use simple statements that won't play down your hard-earned expertise. Don't deliberately diminish your know-how. Exhibit confidence in yourself, and others will do likewise.

Sssssssh: power in silence

Ironically, inserting silence into your communications is one of the most powerful ways to be heard. In many cases, if we're talking constantly, in the same tone, at the same speed, we present as predictable, formulaic and bland.

Do your best not to talk for the sake of it. By speaking valuable content, at times that really demand it, we'll have far greater potential to cut through the clutter to elicit a response. Don't rush to fill the void. Silence and pauses are like white space in design – they allow all other elements to shine. Embrace silence and speak up when you've got some gold to share with the rest of the room.

After years of observation, I believe the defining characteristic of the 'classic' corporate professional is confidence in their capacity and entitlement to be heard. If you want more impact and influence, pay close attention to the traits of leaders around you – their lack of apologetic language, their signals of self-assuredness, their absence of 'pitching up', their commanding volume and tone. At the executive level, the most impressive leaders use simple, powerful language and are genuinely at ease with silence. Language can strengthen or weaken our presence and personal brand. It's about knowing what signals we're sending, editing and optimising as we go.

Thinking on your feet

We all know the feeling. We're sitting in on a meeting feeling like a low-level imposter and – boom! – we're ambushed. With a racing heart rate, we're asked to say something by the CEO, or cued into a conversation in a way we're not expecting. This is where our window of opportunity is live. Remembering we're 'seen in soundbites', it's not the time to be paralysed. Don't be a newsreader who fails to deliver the genuine headline. When we literally have a live audience listening to us and we bury the lead content, we've lost an opportunity to talk about what we're working on, why it's important to us, how we're making a difference and, essentially, to showcase why we're valuable! Why, then, would our audience pay attention next time?

The first 30 seconds of any news story are critical in capturing the audience's attention and keeping them with you thereafter. This is no different to any of us pitching to clients or delivering a presentation at work. I constantly hear women saying they simply can't 'PR' themselves. Let me set you straight on this one – laying down the facts about yourself or your work is not in any way a shameless exercise in self-promotion. It's an evidence-based report about how much money you're adding to the profit margin of your company.

So the next time you're ambushed, don't panic: pull focus. If you have two minutes to communicate your best work, see if following the Headline > Info > Close out framework helps you organise your thoughts so you can step into the meeting with confidence and control.

Headline > Info > Close out

1. Headline

- Get clear on the headline. What's the *real* headline here – not the headline that is most relevant to you, but the one that is most important to your audience?
- Be firm, be bold and embrace the moment you have to share what's important to you, your audience and the particular moment at hand.
- I suggest one idea and one sentence. Are you presenting a challenge, have you discovered an obstacle for the team, can you start with a quick poll to read the room and grab attention?

2. Info

- Have three strong facts. Find your facts – fall back on evidence that your work has produced. For example, if you've introduced a new initiative that has generated a 60% increase in sales this quarter, then say so.
- Use statistics and hard data to reinforce your point.
- Keep to one idea per sentence. If you have three different sets of data, then give them one line each, and be sure to verbally signpost as you go, for example "tactic 1…, tactic 2…, tactic 3 …".
- You must guide your audience through your communications. Fail to navigate and you'll fail to engage and retain them.

3. Close out

- How are you closing? What do you want the audience to do about this information right now? What challenges or opportunities does it reveal? Have you brought them a breakthrough in some form and if so, what do you need them to act on in the next 24 hours?

- What's likely to happen in the market if they *don't* act?
- Be specific about what you need and give the audience a sense of urgency if you can.
- Close with a compelling, clear call to action.

This framework can be used (at least in some form) across every context of your work. From meetings and emails, to keynotes, phone calls, or passing commentary with your boss – adopt this model to organise your thoughts, and think on your feet at breakneck speed. If you have time to prepare – bonus. Find the latest data, gather market intelligence, talk to your peers – sharpen every step of the process when time is on your side.

Here's an example. Say I work for a real estate agency and I'm giving my team an update.

Headline

"Morning team, I've called this meeting because we're behind our target by 30%. There are three things I'd like us to do this week to hit our mark for the developer."

Info

1. *Double check that you're following up with clients who have registered to inspect one of the properties.*
2. *Call and book them in for an inspection and briefing.*
3. *Report back to me as soon as anyone wants to proceed with a sale.*

Close out

To summarise: this is a challenging market, and we only have two weeks to close on the last four apartments before the developer hands it over to another agent. So we're all on notice, and we're all expected to action today's three-point plan. Are there any questions?"

This is an abbreviated example, but you can clearly see that by following a simple, tidy framework, you make it easy for the audience to understand you. The content will be different for every audience, and it may well be a 20-minute report, but the framework remains the same. Highlight the critical content, be interesting, be clear on your closing 'want' and have impact.

I urge you to use this framework when the phone rings and the conversation is important. Once you're in the swing of this, you'll do it on auto-pilot. When you're next ambushed by the CEO or someone important in your network, you'll rest confident in your ability to organise your thoughts and think on your feet. Armed with both a short report framework and a comprehensive understanding of how to use your voice, body language and language, I'd like you to record yourself delivering this on your smartphone and see what kind of impact you have. Employ this framework once a week, and before you know it, you'll be flying. You'll notice your elevated presence and credibility, and others will too.

Do it with swagger: the trifecta effect

Oprah, President Bill Clinton, the Dalai Lama. Their names alone are enough to generate a response, so you can appreciate the intensity of sharing a room with them. It's a little like being caught in the gravitational force of a small planet. I can thank a career in journalism for these out-of-body experiences. So, what did I learn from the privilege of their presence? Everything you have just read. Through years of practice, these captivating communicators have all mastered what I refer to as the 'trifecta effect' – when voice, body language and use of language are mastered individually and used together for impact.

As you can see, we can all 'channel the trifecta' to command a boardroom, an investor presentation, a pay-rise pitch or ad-hoc office gathering, by simply taking control of the signals we're sending. As a facilitator, I have spent years leading communication workshops – as well as media training many high-ranking CEOs from ASX-listed companies.

These are core enterprise skills we *all* need to work on. Not just mid-career professionals, but top executives committed to connecting with their audience need to routinely block time in their overloaded schedule to refine and rehearse each of the simple tactics shared in this chapter. Leaders take communication skills as seriously as other parts of their role. I have seen remarkable turnarounds in confidence and capability at the highest level, but only because these high-flyers have recognised that speaking with impact can be learned, if you're up for the work.

When we have a window of opportunity to connect with our audience we either build or detract from our personal brand. Communication is the foundation of our brand and our business relationships. For some of us, this means taking more risk and speaking up, or perhaps simply speaking louder. For many middle-aged women in particular this can be confronting. We're used to an environment where women assume the 'support' position at work. Competing without feeling ashamed of this often perceived 'unattractive' quality is not part of an office culture that we're necessarily at ease with. This is precisely where we need to defy a programmed instinct to please and take risks to rewire our unconscious behaviour. In this way, we can start putting ourselves on a level playing field instead of waiting for a 'more appropriate' one to arrive.

The rules of engagement here are simple: park the emotion you attach to fear and risk, and advocate for what you want. Communicate what you need. Identify the gaps and upskill accordingly. And if you really want to be in the game of #FutureFIT career growth, then rely on you, and only you, to make the change you want to see.

Tapping into adaptability

"Perhaps technology is revealing more clearly to us now what has always been a truth: that everyone has something rare and powerful to offer our society, and that the human ability to adapt is our greatest asset."

—AIMEE MULLINS, ATHLETE, ADVOCATE, ACTOR

We all know someone who can't use an Excel spreadsheet or who can't text message proficiently or even open a PDF on their smartphone. I have also come across people (of a slightly older generation) who don't *want* to understand how to do any of the above. Even when the Apple store holds regular and free workshops for those struggling to use the technology, they stubbornly refuse to adapt to systems that are second nature to everyone around them. Yes mum, I'm looking at you!

Our environment is changing. Other people are changing and technology is constantly changing. If we can't accept and adapt to change in ourselves, we'll create a dislocation between ourselves and our community, where the longer we stay stuck the harder it will be to catch up. There is scientific research behind adaptability being a necessary trait for a good leader, which I would argue has relevance to anyone who is part of a community – because we are all leaders whether we know it or not. We are all role modelling an ability to either embrace change, or allow it to level us.

In 1987, *The New York Times* ran a story titled, 'The Battle of the Spreadsheets'. By today's standards it's not exactly clickbait, but at the time it was big news: the first clash between two software giants, Microsoft and Lotus. Lotus was the heavyweight champion of spreadsheets. Its program – Lotus 1-2-3 – was a killer app. People bought PCs just so they could use that one program. And Microsoft? It had decided to take on Lotus 1-2-3 with a little program called Excel. You don't need me to tell you who won that battle. Safe to say Lotus now sits alongside side-ponytails and leg-warmers in the eighties graveyard.

Lotus knew Excel was coming and it didn't do anything until it was too late. It thought Lotus 1-2-3 was untouchable and instead key clients left in droves to adopt Excel. The thing was, Lotus could have acted. It could have built an app that was compatible with Microsoft's Windows. In other words, it could have adapted. It's easy to think of Lotus as a cautionary tale. And don't get me wrong, it definitely is. None of us wants to be a Lotus in our own lives. But it's not the whole story. The pace of change that Lotus was contending with when Excel came in is nothing compared to what each and every one of us faces today. Excel was a snail. Today, change comes at us like a wave. And like waves, it keeps coming.

But you knew that already. It's why you're reading this book. There's no sticking our heads in the sand Lotus-style around here. But just because we know what's coming doesn't make it any easier. That's why this chapter is so important. I'm going to put it out there, it might even be the *most* important of the eight human skills I talk about in this book. I see being adaptable as the foundational mindset essential for not only dealing with change, but thriving through it. We can't go with the flow here, because that flow is going to knock our feet out from under us. Being adaptable will not only enable you to keep your feet on the ground, it will help you march those feet right to the front of the change space.

Unnatural selection

Humans are great adaptors, maybe even the best. Just take a quick mental trip around the world and look at all the different climates and environments that we manage to live in. Indeed, until very recently all our human endeavours have been entirely concentrated on altering our immediate surroundings to tip the likelihood of survival a little further in our favour. A quick note before I continue: this is by no means a lesson in biology, but it's worth spending a bit of time considering the formative role that adaptability has played in making us who we are – and the challenges that same evolutionary process now presents.

The moment we learned to walk upright and expanded our field of view, we bought ourselves that little bit of extra time to spot predators in the distance. And by process of natural selection, we carried these biological adaptations forward. With survival still at the forefront of our primitive brains, we used that extra time pretty well. First up: learning to use tools and harnessing fire to, among other things, ensure we got the sustenance we needed to power our big brains.

Then, for reasons that aren't entirely understood, about 100,000 years ago our particular brand of human – Homo sapiens – leapt to the top of the food chain. As explained by Noah Yuval Harari in his book *Sapiens: A Brief History of Humankind*, we've basically been wreaking havoc ever since:

"Humankind ascended to the top so quickly that the ecosystem was not given time to adjust. Most top predators of the planet are majestic creatures. Millions of years of dominion have filled them with self-confidence. Sapiens by contrast is more like a banana-republic dictator."

'Little c' and 'big C' change

Let's pause our biology lesson briefly to look at why adaptability has shot to the top of the #FutureFIT list. If adaptability is so hard-baked into us as humans, what competitive advantage does it really offer in the future of work?

The reason is adaptability's best frenemy: change. So far, still not surprising. As we've seen, change has always been a part of life and in our more recent history, a part of work. Because of this, we've always had to adapt and just as we honed our skills to life on the savanna, so too did we hone our skills in the workplace, albeit over a much shorter time frame. For a few relatively stable decades, we adapted to life in workplaces characterised by command and control structures and linear career paths. And then everything changed.

Right now, Yuval's Sapiens-led banana republic is facing unprecedented challenges of our own creation. Ever since we cemented our place as predator number one, we've worked to shorten the cycle of innovation. Let's put to one side the fact that it took our evolutionary ancestors hundreds of thousands of years to fully exploit the benefits of fire (i.e. to cook food). In much more recent history, the number of years it takes for new technology to be adopted has been steadily, or perhaps unsteadily, decreasing. The reason, as noted by Nick Davis, Vice President of Corporate Innovation at Singularity University, is that each new technology builds on existing exponential technologies:

"Consider the telephone, a game-changing technology in its day. It actually took 75 years for landline phone usage to reach 50 million users...

"Compare that to the adoption of mobile phones, which took 12 years to reach the 50 million user mark. It's remarkable that Pokémon GO reached 50 million users in just 19 days, but that feat was only possible because the game is built on top of other exponential technologies, including computer processing power, mobile phones, the internet, and augmented reality."

In his book *Thank You for Being Late*, Thomas Friedman explains this acceleration via a graph drawn by Eric 'Astro' Teller, Captain of Moonshots (aka CEO) of Alphabet's secret squirrel research company, X. Teller's graph plots the rate of tech-driven innovation against the rate of human adaptability. While the human line tracks along at a sedate, linear pace, the technology line curves up exponentially, passing and then accelerating away from the rate of human adaptability. At a point shortly after the technology line starts to curve away from the adaptability line, Teller drew a dot and marked it "we are here". His point is that while humans have always adapted to their surroundings, and will continue to, most of us can no longer keep pace with the rate of technological change. We're being left behind.

And OK, so Teller's graph isn't exactly statistically sound, with some people pointing out that, according to Teller, the answer to bridging the gap between technology and human adaptability is time travel. But the point remains: humans have never before had to adapt this quickly. And as we see the technology train (to use an appropriately outdated metaphor) speed off into the distance we are left feeling disoriented and out of control. This latter aspect is particularly poignant, because it's always been our ability to exert control over our surroundings – harnessing the power of fire, domesticating animals, replacing human labour with machines in the first industrial revolution – that has propelled us forward. Now it's set to hold us back unless we can find a way to speed up our innate ability to adapt.

My former career as a journalist provides a real-life example of the Teller paradox, what I think of as the battle between 'little c' change and 'big C' change. On the ground as a news correspondent, I was constantly dealing with 'little c' change. Breaking news and relentless deadlines meant I was forever adjusting my priorities. I'd moderate my demeanor to suit the assignment and choose my words to match the context. The tone I'd adopt to fire a question on gun control at a White House spokesperson would be entirely inappropriate and upsetting to a survivor of a mass shooting; two very different contexts required two very different Andreas.

Dealing with these everyday challenges required constant micro-adaptations mentally, physically and emotionally. My ability to make these adaptations as seamlessly as possible was based on all the experiences and learnings I had taken on in my career to that date. I might not have known all the changes I might face on any given day, but their general flavour was known to me and I was confident in my ability to adapt my response.

Consider in contrast, today's journalists who have a new colleague in the newsroom: AI or artificial intelligence. Actually, this colleague is not even that new anymore. Natural language generation platform Wordsmith by Automated Insights has been crunching financial reports and pumping out sports coverage for the Associated Press for years. Meanwhile, Reuters announced in 2018 that it was developing a tool called Lynx Insight in pursuit of a "cybernetic" newsroom.

This sci-fi sounding name describes a new journalistic partnership between human and machine, where the human skills of asking questions and exercising judgment are augmented by technology which analyses trends, spots errors and even makes suggestions on what stories to write. That's right. Today's journalist receives tips not from an anonymous human source, but from a robot. That's 'big C' change. Change that can't be addressed by switching priorities or modulating your voice. It requires a complete reassessment of how you do your job.

The new 'Q'

If you weren't already on board with how important adaptability is, let's look at some of the key figures and opinions that are currently out there:

- The 2018 *Future of Jobs Report* by the World Economic Forum (WEF) forecasts significant skill instability in the period from 2018 to 2022, with employers expecting that by 2022, there will have been an average shift of 42% in required workforce skills. In short, almost half of the average worker's skill-set will be out of date in three years' time.

- Social research firm McCrindle Research predicts that members of Generation Z (defined as those born between 1995 and 2009) will have 17 jobs over five careers.

- While no one can quite agree on the exact impact that automation will have on jobs, the International Monetary Fund didn't pull any punches when authors of a recent IMF working paper entitled it: 'Should We Fear the Robot Revolution? (The Correct Answer is Yes)'. The IMF also noted that women are at greater risk of losing their jobs to automation than men.

Based on these numbers, adaptation reliant on generational change isn't going to cut it as a #FutureFIT skill. And it definitely won't bridge the gap in Astro Teller's graph. Instead, we need to take our standard-issue adaptability and develop it to meet the challenges of tomorrow.

This might be why in recent years, there have been increasing references to an 'adaptability quotient' or AQ. It's the third in a list of Qs that have shaped how we think about work over many years. The first Q was in IQ (intelligence quotient) and for quite some time, it was seen as the most important factor in determining our success at work. That was until Daniel Goleman came along in the 1990s, talking about EQ – our emotional intelligence. Goleman's research showed that it wasn't how smart we are that makes the difference, it's how well we know and manage ourselves and others that differentiates the best from the rest.

Then in 2018, Natalie Fratto writing in *Fast Company* took it right up to EQ with an article titled 'Screw Emotional Intelligence – Here's The Key To The Future Of Work'. Those are fighting words for sure. Fratto imagined a future in which your AQ score determined your career, with those scoring highly taking the 'salaried track' which promised a three-year contract with an employer and guaranteed retraining every one to six months.

From where we stand right now, Fratto's vision is galling. For today's tertiary students – many of whom will be acquiring significant HELP debts as they attain their multi-year qualifications – the idea of retraining every one to six months is, frankly, exhausting and possibly financially prohibitive. For mid-career workers, the prospect is perhaps even more daunting. And it will only get worse the longer we stand still. We need to start adapting today.

The adaptable mindset

While the term AQ makes for a nice bit of management-speak, what does it really mean to be #FutureFIT adaptable? Put simply, adaptability is about responding to our environment. But we humans don't really do simple. This is especially the case when it comes to work, where our sense of 'who we are' is often closely entwined with, even indistinguishable from, 'what we do.' Exhibit A: that age-old opening line, "So Andrea, what do you do?"

As a result, we can't see adaptability as a simple equation where our response is the product of emotionless, cognitive inputs. That's why I think AQ requires a mindset that recognises and engages our cognitive and emotional responses to change. In particular, I think there are three perspectives that we should draw on to shape and grow a positive adaptable mindset – described in the Engage > Activate > Release framework below.

Engage > Activate > Release

1. Engage

We can't adapt to change if we don't see it coming (or worse, hide from it when we do). People with a high AQ will proactively engage with what's going on – not just within their industry, but with the world more broadly. They will cultivate a curious and open mind and become a collector of diverse perspectives. And they will be vigilant, ever alert to the signals of change.

2. Activate

Once the bells of change start ringing (again), we need to activate our energy and optimism for change. This is about seeing change as a good thing, as a new path forward. It's about recognising the opportunities that change presents, rather than dwelling on the negatives.

3. Release

Adapting to change inevitably requires movement and to keep moving forward we have to let go of anything that might hold us back. Maybe your ego is bruised because you tried something out and it didn't work. Maybe it's fear over what comes next. We need to be resilient enough to take the hit and humble enough to admit it's OK to cut our losses and move on. People with a high AQ will release themselves from these emotional restraints, opening up their headspace for the challenges ahead.

There are three features of the Engage > Activate > Release framework that I want to call out. First, each perspective involves actively making a choice to see the positives of big change. The enemy of adaptability is passivity. For some people this will be easy – every time a door closes a window opens, that sort of thing. For many others, it will be really hard to continually face change. We have to reckon with the full range of reactions and emotions that change brings out in us (more on that later).

Second, you might notice that these three perspectives involve a lot of mental gymnastics and little in the way of definitive action. This is where we have to see the #FutureFIT skills as a complete toolkit. An adaptable mindset is the secret sauce that flavours your actions with purpose and potency in an otherwise ambiguous and changing landscape. In particular, it will guide the steps you take to be a lifelong learner. Learning without a specific purpose is a hobby – which has its own value of course – but in the future of work we have to use our AQ to shape our learning, our networks and the way we lead ourselves and others.

Third, the only way to get onboard with these perspectives is to believe you can improve your AQ. In the well-cited words of Carol Dweck, you need to have a growth mindset about your capacity to adapt. Each of us will come from different AQ starting points; different levels of comfort when it comes to dealing with change. Adapting a growth mindset is a starting point that through effort can be cultivated and expanded.

Boost your AQ: Part 1

Seek out (really) different perspectives

It's easy to pat yourself on the back because you asked someone in another function or industry for their perspective on an issue. Consult diverse stakeholders? Tick. But guess what? Most of the time we still approach people that we feel aligned to in some way, which means their perspective may not be as different as we think. Find ways to connect with people outside your usual circles – not just in your work, but socially, politically and culturally. Challenge yourself to really listen to their opinions and interrogate how and why they might differ from your own. How might your particular experiences have shaped your view? What privileges do you bring? What experiences and viewpoints are you missing?

See 'little c' change as a rehearsal for the 'big C' show

Don't always shoot straight for the solution when you encounter a problem or hit resistance. Going straight into solution mode is a missed opportunity to think about what else is out there. Take a step back and ask, "What caught me out here?" "What surprised me?" "What would it look like if we aimed for the edge of possibility rather than the safe middle?"

Don't be afraid to admit when things aren't working with your team. Instead, call it out and ask how you could do things differently. Becoming more comfortable with the push and pull of change will give you the emotional and mental scaffolding to take on bigger and bigger challenges.

Build up your silver linings bank account

Everyone from your parents to your year nine teacher and your swimming coach will have encouraged you to learn from your mistakes. And they were right – analysing what went wrong and what you could do differently can uncover absolute personal development gold. But with change coming at us at an unprecedented rate, we also need to feed our resilience stores. So when you collect those lessons from your experiences, collect not only the development points but the silver linings as well – the things that went well, the things you did well and the things you just felt damn good about. Think about it as making deposits in your silver linings bank account that you can draw on when facing your next challenge or when you feel beaten up by change.

Adaptability in action

It's easy to find corporate examples of adaptability. Airbnb and PayPal both made major pivots early on although Netflix perhaps takes the cake. The streaming service started life (over 20 years ago!) as a subscription service. One of its early victories was leveraging the resources of the US Postal Service to fulfil orders. While the internet was always the end game, Netflix really showed its adaptability chops in 2007. It was just weeks away from releasing its own hardware when CEO Reed Hastings made the decision to pull the release. Instead, Netflix starting partnering with other hardware makers to embed their software in those machines, paving the way for it to become the streaming superpower of today.

The Netflix story is a cracking example of adaptability in action. But while Hastings was no doubt deeply and personally invested in the success of the business, I wanted to learn more about individual experiences of adaptability. I reached out to my friend Dr Catherine Ball, Australia's 'Dame of Drones', and wearer of many hats including entrepreneur, author, executive director and ethics advocate.

On the day we speak, Ball, together with her husband, has just launched the website for her latest business. This takes her current tally of businesses to five. That's current total, not absolute total – that number is nine. It's this part of Ball's story that interests me most, how's she navigated the ups and downs of startup life and how she's adapted along the way. She starts by telling me about how she sets intentions, a more values-forward alternative to traditional goal-setting.

> "For me, an intention is your true north, the touchstone you come back to again and again to assess where you're at. We get so caught up in the journey that we forget about the destination. I think to be truly adaptable, we need to reframe our thinking about the destination. Of course, that destination is no longer about a specific job, career or business model. It's about where we want to be more broadly and, importantly, how we want to feel. Especially looking five, ten years into the future, it's all about how you want to feel rather than the specifics of what you'll be doing. How you actually get there is unlikely to be a direct line. It's unlikely to go how you think it's going to go. That's certainly been the case for me."

Staying true to the intentions Ball has set for herself has helped her make the difficult decisions she's needed to make along the way.

> "Recently, I had to kill one of the things I had been singing about for the last two years. But there's a saying that goes something like: 'when you get to the end of your life, you've got to look at how well you've lived, how well you've loved and how well you've learned to let go'. Well, letting things go has been one of the hardest things I've had to come to terms with but it has to be done if you're going to adapt. I still take things personally. I put my heart and soul into things. But if it's not working, it's not working. Close it."

While that particular business no longer exists, Ball's intention lives on and has been reborn in a new venture, with a new business model. The fact that Ball's intention is independent of any one business iteration is the critical point: "I let go of the business, but I don't let go of the intention," explains Ball. "I kept the gold and got rid of all the extraneous stuff that was preventing that gold from shining."

Because of this, Ball doesn't carry the four businesses she's closed around with her like dead weight. They're all necessary stopovers as she keeps moving onwards towards her destination. And they're definitely not failures. "There's no such thing as failure," says Ball, the second that I utter that particular F word. "I met a woman once, who was deeply into yoga and spirituality. She told me that when she first heard the word 'namaste', she thought the person was saying 'no mistakes'. So she was like 'yes! no mistakes!' and I love that. So if I ever have the time to go to yoga, I'm think 'yes! no mistakes!' "

Boost your AQ: Part 2

Be intentional about your intentions

Take Ball's lead and set intentions that will provide a framework for the adaptive choices you make and actions you take over a specific timeframe.

- **Make your intention positive.** Think, "My intention is to be in a role that challenges me and aligns to my passion for teaching" rather than, "My intention is to still have a job".

- **Consider setting short-term and long-term intentions.** A long-term intention can be your guiding light, but think about how short-term intentions can help focus you day-to-day on what matters. If your long-term intention is as above, a short-term intention may be around finding ways to experience how AI is being used in classrooms.

- **Check-in with yourself.** For those of us schooled in SMART goals, intentions can seem a little non-specific. But that's partially the point. Instead of ticking a box, take a few minutes to connect to your intention and make sure your daily activities continue to reflect the values and aspirations it represents.

Let your intentions guide experimentation

I've already mentioned using intentions to guide your actions, but there's one specific type of action that intentions can give real purpose to: experimentation. Trying things out is a critical adaptability skill. Whether something works or not, it's all useful data in building your #FutureFIT self. The specifics of the experiments you might want to try will be discussed in more detail in other chapters. Here, it's enough to think about how your intentions can help liberate you from the fear of failure and instead embrace a "no mistakes!" mentality.

Hold yourself to account

In her book *Mindset: The New Psychology of Success*, Carol Dweck doesn't pull any punches when she challenges us to hold ourselves accountable in adopting a growth mindset:

> "People are all born with a love of learning, but the fixed mindset can undo it. Think of a time you were enjoying something – doing a crossword puzzle, playing a sport, learning a new dance. Then it became hard and you wanted out. Maybe you suddenly felt tired, dizzy, bored or hungry. Next time this happens, don't fool yourself. It's the fixed mindset. Put yourself in a growth mindset. Picture your brain forming new connections as you meet the challenge and learn. Keep on going."

The same goes for the effort required to increase your AQ. Don't let your eyes glaze over the suggested activities in this book – it's the fixed mindset holding you back.

That said, be kind to yourself

Holding yourself to account doesn't mean you need to be a martyr to change. Keeping up with the speed of change is a relentless task and it won't be easing off any time soon. We all need ways to help deal with this, from ensuring we have a supportive community around us, to devoting time to 'slow' activities – like reading, bingeing a Netflix series or just going outside for a walk.

Train your brain

We started this chapter with a very brief sojourn into our biological origins. We're going to finish it by looking at the biological promise that our (now thoroughly evolved) brains offer in our efforts to become more adaptable.

We've talked a lot about how adaptability is about respond-ing to changes in context, whether they be 'big C' or 'little c' changes. The specific part of the brain that lights up when it comes to dealing with different situations is the hippocampus, which according to Richard J. Davidson in *Building Blocks of Emotional Intelligence: Adaptability: A Primer* encodes the context in which events occur. These become specific cues in our environment and we learn to respond to these cues in an "appropriate and skilful" way.

This "appropriate and skilful" response is the essence of adaptability. So if you want to build your AQ, you need to get your hippocampus firing. And there are some very interesting developments in the study of neuroplasticity that suggest the hippocampus is particularly well – dare I say it – adapted to making neuroplastic changes. Davidson explains that the hippocampus is different from other brain regions because it's where "neurogenesis" takes place, it's where new brain cells grow. Neurogenesis "definitively can occur in the hippocampus, and may occur in other parts of the brain. The one thing known to non-pharmacologically increase the number of brain cells in the hippocampus, to promote neurogenesis, is aerobic exercise. Aerobic exercise will stimulate the growth of new neurons, new brain cells, in the hippocampus."

Before you put down this book and head out on a run, Davidson hastens to add that it's not quite that simple: "... plasticity in and of itself is not necessarily good. It's neutral. Plasticity may be good, but if you're in a very toxic environment and you increase your neuroplasticity, it may make things worse because you are more effectively encoding that toxic input."

In addition, the enemy of the hippocampus is the stress hor-mone cortisol. The hippocampus is particularly well endowed with cortisol receptors, so when our adrenal glands start shooting cortisol into our bloodstream in response to a stressful event, it's the hippocampus that really cops it. So much so, that over a prolonged period the cumulative effect of all that cortisol can actually cause cell death. Not words you want to hear ever, and especially not in relation to your brain. Davidson makes the obvious link to adaptability: "The more stressed you are over time, the less adaptable you are. Therefore, things that reduce stress can help people be more adaptable."

So it seems biology still has a few tricks up its sleeve when it comes to our continuing capacity to adapt. It's time to evolve again and unleash our full adaptive potential.

Nurturing creativity

"The mental skill that is the last remaining competitive advantage an individual or organisation can have in today's technologically-driven world – a skill that machines have not been able to replicate – is mental flexibility, or also known as creativity." —TODD SAMPSON

Creativity will be the key driver of growth in the future of work, because businesses are facing more complex problems as they enter new markets and new sectors where competition is coming from unexpected places. When we engage creativity in ourselves, we can generate ideas, identify new opportunities and solve complex problems.

Creativity is the engine of innovation. If we're to stay relevant, this is a human skill we need to understand and invest in. We need to explore the difference between 'big C' creativity like Edison and Einstein and the everyday 'small c' creativity – why the mind needs to exercise its autonomy and how we can develop a creative mindset to solve the problems we face across our industries.

Old school, new (creative) tricks

Don't hesitate to contact me with an experience to the contrary, but I don't believe anybody ever received Dux of School X for being exceptionally creative. No one ever received a scholarship for it either. There have been scholarships for academic excellence, music, sport or potentially 'the arts', of course, but most certainly never for 'creative intelligence' in and of itself. When I recall the first day of my final year of high school – a standard late January Queensland stinker – I jump immediately to the Principal's welcome address; a charming reiteration of the significance of the months to come, that would land each of us a numerical intellectual ranking to make or break our tertiary destiny, and ultimately, our success in life. Yikes. What a system.

I've always considered myself to be somewhat creative by nature, but by no means a 'creative' per se. 'Creatives' are the truly talented people who engage in creative pursuits for a living: the designers, producers, painters, directors, architects, musicians and artisans. They are those born with an inherent ability to produce wonderfully original, artistic, thought-provoking, desirable 'things' to be admired, consumed and enjoyed. Right?

In preparing for this chapter – one eliciting particular intrigue and excitement – I came to realise that 'creativity' brings with it a hefty slew of preconceived ideas, expectations and definitions. Creativity is an almost utopian attribute among us humans; revered by many, but truly embraced, mastered and celebrated by few. Indeed, perhaps its perceived relative 'scarcity' is all part of its appeal.

At the onset, I was pretty confident in my understanding of creativity, its relevance to the future of work and the value it offers us individuals developing it. As I began to scratch the surface, however, I discovered a body of work far deeper than I ever imagined; one rich with psychological, sociological, educational and economic significance – both for now and into the future. I discovered a discipline on the verge of transforming traditional learning, talent acquisition and development frameworks, of turning them on their (somewhat archaic) head.

Got a brain? Read on...

If you're a self-confessed STEM-focused (that's science, technology, engineering and mathematics), left brain operating individual, you most certainly do *not* have an excuse to skip this chapter. Creativity's place in the future of work isn't confined to the graphic designers, creative directors, producers, photographers, artisans, teachers and other 'heroes of humanities'. Quite the opposite. While traditional constructs of creativity have often forced a division of those who either are, or are not, creatively inclined, research points to the potential in every human being to be creative – at least to some degree.

So gather round, because in this chapter you'll learn that creativity is a non-negotiable lever to your future success. What's more, you'll discover creativity is an asset we all have the ability to strengthen and apply in our everyday lives, almost immediately. Read quickly, however, as the older we get, the less open we are to the prospect of change. Eeek!

As we've explored already, the future is set to be one marked by exceptional change. By 2022, the skills required to perform most jobs will have shifted significantly. In fact, the WEF's *Future of Jobs* forecast to 2022 tells us workers will see an average shift of 42% in required workplace skills in the period leading up to 2022. Skills growing in prominence include analytical thinking and active learning, alongside technology design and upskilling across STEM in accordance with technological developments at large.

However, proficiency in new technologies is only one part of the future skills equation. From all the research, white papers, talks, podcasts, books and blogs I've trawled in recent times, by far the most compelling, consistently published insight around 'the future of work' continues to be the increasing demand for the essence of what it means to live, breathe, feel, see, smell, touch, relate, engage and think; the essence of being human. By 'human', I'm of course pointing to the very characteristics and qualities that our beating hearts and buzzing brains bring to our day-to-day roles; those which (to date) are irreplaceable by code, algorithm, robot or machine.

Alongside the WEF, McKinsey's *Jobs lost, jobs gained: Workforce transitions in a time of automation* white paper tells us workers of the future will spend more time on activities that machines are less capable of: managing people, applying expertise and communicating with others. They will spend less time on predictable physical activities and on collecting and processing data, where machines already exceed human performance. We'll all require heightened social and emotional skills, and advanced cognitive capabilities such as logical reasoning and creativity. CREATIVITY. That's right – from here on in, human skills such as creativity, originality, initiative and critical thinking are set to retain or increase their value.

But it's not just forensic data forecasts exposing the growing importance of 'human' skills and creativity in particular. In 2017, leading consulting firm PwC published compelling anecdotal accounts from CEOs across the world in its 20th annual global CEO survey. The survey revealed that 77% of CEOs struggle to find the creativity and innovation skills they need, and while STEM and digital skills were acknowledged as important, demand for these was outstripped by traditionally 'soft' skills like creativity. CEOs undoubtedly see the value in technology, yet know its true potential hinges on a harmonious interplay with exclusively human capabilities. The skills CEOs consider to be most important are those that can't be replicated by machines – the uniquely human capabilities that stimulate innovation.

Brain systems: a speedy science lesson

As our #FutureFIT action list takes shape, creativity, it seems, should be floating atop the page. Leading global authorities are writing about it, CEOs are calling for it, and furthermore, are concerned about the shortage of it. But let's get back to basics – what does creativity really mean, and what is its value proposition in the context of future-proofing our careers?

"Creativity is like intelligence" says Roger Beaty, Postdoctoral Fellow in Cognitive Neuroscience, Harvard University. "It can be considered a trait that everyone – not just creative 'geniuses' like Picasso and Steve Jobs – possesses in some capacity."

Often defined as the ability to come up with new and useful ideas, creativity is not just your ability to paint a picture or design a dress. We all call on creativity to function in our daily lives, whether it's concocting dinner from leftovers or crafting a 'new look' from existing wardrobe staples. Creative tasks range from what researchers call 'little c' creativity – developing a website, crafting a birthday card or scheming a funny joke – to 'big C' creativity – penning a board report, composing a speech or designing a scientific experiment. Recent evidence also suggests that creativity involves a complex interplay between spontaneous and controlled thinking – the ability to both brainstorm ideas on the fly, and consciously evaluate them to determine whether they're actually viable.

Clearly then, creativity holds a pervasive and powerful place in both our personal and professional worlds. That said, it must be noted that we're not all creatively equal. Degrees of creative capability certainly exist.

In a recent study, Beaty and his colleagues examined whether a person's creative thinking ability can be explained, in part, by a connection between three specific brain systems: the default, salience and executive networks. The default network activates when we engage in spontaneous thinking, such as mind-wandering, daydreaming and imagining. This network may play a key role in idea development or brainstorming – devising several potential solutions to a problem. The executive control network activates when we need to focus or control our thoughts. This network may play a key role in idea evaluation, reviewing whether brainstormed ideas will actually work, and modifying them to fit the creative objective. The salience network acts as a switching mechanism between the default and executive networks. This network may play a key role in alternating between idea generation and idea evaluation.

Beaty's findings revealed a whole-brain network associated with high creative ability comprised the cortical hubs within default, salience and executive systems – intrinsic functional networks that tend to work in opposition. This suggested that particularly creative people are characterised by their ability to simultaneously engage these three large-scale brain networks. The research also revealed that a person's level of creativity could be predicted – albeit modestly – by the strength of their connections in this triple-thread network. Overall, people with stronger connections came up with better ideas. Interestingly, these three networks typically don't activate at the same time. For example, when the executive network is activated, the default network is usually switched off. Simply put, particularly creative people are better able to co-activate brain networks that usually work separately.

What this research did not explore, however, was whether these networks were malleable or relatively fixed. For example, would a semester of life drawing classes enhance the connectivity within these networks of my brain? The jury is out.

The ROI and why it all matters

We've explored a little of the science behind creativity and why – physiologically – some people may be more creative than others, but what about its application and relevance to the future of work? With CEOs crying out for it, surely there's a meaningful association to be drawn between creativity, professional success and the big wide world of commercial bottom lines? You bet. So much so, that multinational powerhouses like Adobe have even conducted their own research to stress the need for creative skills and capacities in their recruits.

On the eve of the Adobe MAX 2016 event, Adobe released global survey findings that revealed investing in creativity absolutely pays off, with tangible benefits – from higher income to greater national competitiveness and productivity. Independently produced by Edelman Intelligence, the *State of Create: 2016* study surveyed 5,026 adults (18+ years of age) in the US, UK, France, Germany and Japan. The findings were vast, with the following insights particularly pertinent to our #FutureFIT game plan:

- Those (US respondents) who identify as creators report household income 13% higher than non-creators.

- More than two-thirds believe that creative people make better workers, leaders, parents and students.

- Being creative drives self-worth; creators are more likely than non-creators to identify themselves as innovative, confident, problem solvers and happy.

- Despite the above, only 55% of respondents described themselves as creative, and moreover, **only 44% say they're living up to their creative potential**.

Adobe's study exposed the ROI of creativity beyond individual perks too – businesses enjoy equally impressive benefits from prioritising creativity and good design:

- Most (US) respondents believe businesses that invest in creativity are more likely to foster innovation, be competitive, provide better customer experience, have satisfied customers and be financially successful.

- Respondents also believed such businesses are more likely to have happier employees and increased employee productivity.

- 83% agree there is increasing pressure to be productive rather than creative at work. **However, 62% say people are increasingly expected to think creatively at work.**

Eyeballing the list of findings, I wasn't surprised by the alarmist address from Mala Sharma, vice president and general manager of Adobe Creative Cloud, which came with it: "Creativity and productivity go hand in hand, but investing in creativity isn't on the agenda for enough of today's leaders. This survey provides a big wake-up call to businesses that they need to think differently and give employees the tools and freedom to be creative."

Use it or lose it

Pieces of the creative puzzle are starting to align, but some glaring gaps remain. Future of work forecasts and global CEO anecdotes point to creativity as a growing #FutureFIT skill, and research commissioned by big business confirms its undeniable commercial value, yet the same research also indicates our creative capability remains largely under-indexed. How, then, can we better unleash our creative potential? How can we better tap the creative talents we all possess, at least to some degree?

I couldn't help but wonder if this was even possible for us 'more mature' humans, bearing the following two simple scientific truths in mind:

- The Law of Least Effort – basically, our brain is fundamentally lazy, or as scientists say, it is 'necessarily efficient'.

- Functional Fixedness – over time we defend more, question less... and in tandem, tend to become increasingly arrogant!

To cut a long story short, for neurological reasons, our creative 'potential' has a tendency to wane with age. Though adult brains are more flexible and volatile than once thought, they're still far less malleable than a teenage brain. Thus, as we age, not only does creativity comes less naturally, but we're more afraid of change, which is not ideal for those of us noticing a new wrinkle each day!

In search of a more optimistic outlook, I headed along to the Radio Alive 2018 conference in Melbourne, and made a beeline for the 'Improving Creativity' keynote from Australia's Todd Sampson. Writer, producer, adventurer and host of multiple award-winning international documentaries including *Redesign My Brain*, Canadian-born Sampson has long championed the power of creativity in many and varied ways: "The mental skill that is the last remaining competitive advantage an individual or organisation can have in today's technologically-driven world – a skill that machines have not been able to replicate – is mental flexibility, or also known as creativity."

It's fair to say I wasn't disappointed that day. In fact, I may have skipped my way out of the auditorium. While Sampson was quick to reference The Law of Least Effort and Functional Fixedness up front, he made clear it wasn't all bad news. "We are born with incredible mental flexibility. There is no biological reason to lose it as we become adults other than lack of use."

Boom! Now *that* is some #FutureFIT gold worth noting. When it comes to mental skill, we need to use it to avoid losing it. With this in mind, what kind of strategies can we use to improve our mental skill – our creativity? According to Sampson, it's all about 'The Big Three': forced adaptation, visualisation and emotional regulation.

'The Big Three'? My inner journalist hit forensic overdrive. What does each mean, and how we can adopt them for heightened creative prowess?

Try this at home... exercises in creativity: Part 1

1. Forced adaptation

Scientists often say that when it comes to brain development, it only happens outside your comfort zone. Forced adaptation follows the exact same concept of resistance as for physical training. Push your brain to explore unfamiliar terrain, and you'll harness creative muscle in the process.

An aside... Exploring this further, I was fascinated to learn that some of history's greatest geniuses were accustomed to adopting bizarrely 'different' work habits. Benjamin Franklin thought he was at his most productive when naked and cold. Igor Stravinsky stood on his head for 15 minutes each morning to "clear his brain". Charles Dickens wrote with a compass by his side so he could be sure he was always facing north. Investor Nikola Tesla would curl his toes 100 times on each foot as a way of stimulating his brain cells. The list goes on. So, are geniuses just more prone to quirky, 'outside comfort zone' habits, or did their quirks fuel their genius? New York based writer Eric Spitznagel was equally fascinated by this. So much so, that he not only investigated the science behind the quirks of some of the greatest brains in history, but put them to the test himself. From 'cold and naked' to 'staying in bed', 'way too much coffee', 'celibacy', 'wearing the same clothes', 'drinking up a storm' and more, the results were cagey at best – the only quirk he was likely to adopt on a regular basis thereafter was writing in bed! Demanding an expert opinion on the matter, Spitznagel queried Scott Barry Kaufman, PhD, the director at the University of Pennsylvania's Imagination Institute. "The key is to put yourself in a space that shifts your thinking. Unusual experiences are good for the brain. Geniuses only seem quirky to others because they don't have trouble risking madness," said Kaufman.

Build it into your #FutureFIT Toolkit

Learning another language, an instrument or sporting code is a great way to improve your creativity through forced adaptation. The same goes for changing up your physical environment. Whether it's frequenting a new coffee spot every weekend, booking a sabbatical overseas, or living that bucket list escape on the Galapagos Islands, there's nothing like shaking the shackles of routine and plunging into the unfamiliar. Travel stimulates new ideas and perspectives and heightens our sense of perception.

2. Visualisation

Why is visualisation so powerful? What you visualise, becomes you. Whether we're swimming in a lake, or only picturing it, we activate many of the same neural networks; paths of interconnected nerve cells that link what you physically do to the brain impulses that control it. Have you ever fantasised that you're a lean, mean running machine, with Churchillian speech-making talents, magnetic charisma and superhuman confidence? If so, then you've already tapped into the tool that can help you get there in real life.

Build it into your #FutureFIT toolkit

Use *all* your senses. Mental imagery is often referred to as visualisation, but you don't need to limit it to visuals. The most effective imagery involves all five senses. What are you smelling, hearing, feeling? You should be so immersed in a mental image that it seems as if it is actually happening. Furthermore, *be the star, not the audience*. To engage in your practice fully, imagine performing the activity from your own perspective – don't watch yourself as if you're viewing a movie.

3. Emotional regulation

Every day, people are continually exposed to a vast array of potentially arousing stimuli. Emotional regulation is a complex process that involves initiating, inhibiting or modulating one's state or behaviour in any given moment – for example the subjective experience (feelings), cognitive responses (thoughts), emotion-related physiological responses (heart rate or hormonal activity) and emotion-related behaviour (bodily actions or expressions). Functionally, emotional regulation can also refer to processes such as the tendency to focus on a task and the ability to suppress inappropriate behaviour.

Build it into your #FutureFIT Toolkit

Jump online and you'll discover a plethora of strategies to work into your everyday routines. In addition to, or as part of, emotional regulation therapy and self-regulation therapy, there are techniques such as meditation, mindfulness and stress management, which can help us to improve our control of negative emotions and response to emotional situations. These techniques can also provide other benefits, like improved mood, heightened ability to focus, and increased feelings of self-worth and empathy.

Phew. Creative fitness can be somewhat optimised by adults after all. Jumping back to the Adobe research, however, I remained unsettled by the overwhelming number of us failing to realise our creative potential. Why was/ is this happening? Beyond the science and the genetic hands we're all dealt, are there environmental and sociological factors at play?

Revisiting my high school and tertiary learning experiences, I had a strong feeling educational frameworks, and traditional socio-cultural measures of 'success' and 'excellence', were part of the equation. It was time for coffee with the master...

In the beginning...

Associate Professor Anne Harris is the Vice Chancellor's Principal Research Fellow at RMIT University's Department of Education – Design and Creative Practice. One of Australia's foremost brains on creativity, Harris' particular focus is the value and place of creativity in the context of educational frameworks.

In recent years, a major part of her work has been an extension of legendary educational psychologist E. Paul Torrance's research into intelligence and creativity in school children.

Torrance established clinical links between fluency, flexibility, original thinking and the ability to elaborate on thoughts as markers for creativity. His creativity index could predict kids' creative accomplishments as adults far better than IQ testing. Harris elaborates:

> "This is an argument we are still making today through our research at RMIT University's School of Education, in developing a national Creativity Index that will measure creative skills and capacities alongside literacy and numeracy. Our research also shows an urgent need for a more ecological approach to improving creativity in schools, not just to measuring it. This means approaching schools as ecosystems in which teachers collaborate with other teachers, students and leadership, and teaching and learning is approached interdisciplinarily."

Flashing back to my high school experience, I was momentarily thrilled at the prospect of it being a dead and buried marker of a bygone era. Momentarily. Harris continued:

> "My general opinion is that education is just completely disengaged as a sector, and almost wholly disengaged from a creativity debate with creative and cultural industries. The understanding that we now increasingly live in a gig economy, and people need more than anything to be flexible and risk-taking and iterative, is completely the opposite ethos and structure of how we measure success in secondary schools.

> "What I first observed and wrote about 10 years ago, is that contemporary education structures in early childhood and primary have always been very 'creatively' strong for structural and developmental reasons. In the last 15–20 years in Australia, it has been prioritised in a

tertiary context or creativity industries and other kinds of changes, developments and emergences, but in compulsory secondary school, it's almost entirely absent. So I asked – why is this gap happening? On the surface we know it's because of standardised testing which is measured along global axes and we want to be globally comparative, but that in some ways is superficial – there are other ways we could do that. It doesn't mean that we need to throw the baby out with the bathwater as it were. There's no reason why we can't do design thinking or other kinds of productive risk taking processes, and value them in secondary context."

Sipping slightly slower on my long black, my excitement around Australia's progressive adoption of a 'Creativity Index' in secondary education was rapidly dwindling. Desperate for answers, I pushed Harris for more.

"The education sector is frightened of progressing this – it's a conservative, slow moving industry. We have a new Australian curriculum and we had the opportunity to address that, and it hasn't been addressed. We have this general capability of creative – it's called creative and critical thinking. That was exciting for a minute because creativity was prioritised, but with the caveat that creativity has trickled into the national curriculum and the work of secondary education in ways that have de-coupled it with the arts and re-coupled it with science and STEM.

"Australia is also really uncomfortable with the 'wankiness' and the elitism of the notion of creativity and 'owning' creativity – we've progressed a little so people can see it in schools as their responsibility, but the mindset shift hasn't happened. It is culturally embedded. In my research experience, Australians are incredibly reluctant to talk about their personal 'creativity', which is why I included other countries in my study. In the US, teachers were most happy to talk about 'What is creativity and how does it manifest in your work?'. Why? Because it's a cultural value in Americans. It's entrepreneurial."

In a recent opinion piece for *The New York Times*, Dr Adam Grant, professor of management and psychology at the Wharton School at the University of Pennsylvania, flagged that "If you always succeed in school, you're not setting yourself up for success in life. Getting straight A's requires conformity. Having an influential career demands originality." I absolutely loved these insights, and was keen for Harris' take. Particularly given that I failed a number of key subjects in Year 12 and, to be consistent, then again at university.

"When I was interviewing a top executive at Google as part of my current study, she said exactly the same thing. The thing I love–hate about the interviews I've done with the higher up multinational leaders is that they can really see the meta perspective – they can absolutely see, and to some degree are orchestrating, the charge in creativity across society. To talk to those people, it's fascinating to see (archaic) national governments and national measures of literacy and numeracy really are almost non-consequential at this point.

"What I heard from the Google exec was that it's really hard in terms of recruiting. Whether they're recruiting from entry-level or senior corporate workers, mostly they're looking for engineers – they know they need those kinds of skills – engineers are always top of their class and have a particular way of thinking. Google wants them because they're over achievers and have a particular wiring, but that alone doesn't work for them. So they have to find that crazy middle place, because they also know that people who've excelled all the way through school have no resilience whatsoever – they have no ability to fail. In Hong Kong for example, where it's not comfortable in school to collaborate, Google was having to hire for specific 'cultural gaps' because the design-thinking/colour-posting sessions in the corporate environment just weren't sticking."

Whether it's surviving the gig economy over the next 40 years, or wanting to land a job at Google, Harris emphasises the need for an understanding that people are looking for different and new ways of being:

"We should be teaching how to curate! When we were little we had to listen to teachers or our parents in order to learn. Kids now just don't. In fact, what they have in their hand is much more powerful because teachers are flawed and limited themselves. Kids are less scared than we are – we're scared because it's clear how quickly the dynamic environment is changing. In fact, it's really exciting – we're in this liminal time right now where people of our (adult) generation were trained to have one job their whole lives, but today's young people never knew it like that. We oldies are a bit pissed off because the terms have changed (we did the right thing, we went to college and now we don't have a job), but for young people, there's actually a lot of freedom in non-linear careers."

In closing our catch-up, I was keen to secure Harris' core 'creativity takeaways' for us as individuals.

"Personal sustainability is critical," says Harris. "Achieving personal sustainability and wellness in an environment that is largely innovation obsessed, is difficult! How do we reframe the expectation of deadline-based output and creativity? In the gig economy, if you can't do it, someone else will. How do you thrive in that over a lifetime? When the design-thinking model is driving us – one laden with deadlines and formulaic based outputs – it generates certain kinds of creativity and innovation, and not necessarily a diversified collection of outputs."

Slowness, says Harris, is the enemy of all of that:

"There are certain kinds of creative developments that take a lot of time, and there's no capacity for that creative ecology now. It has to be 'fast' creativity. Not only is that going to be hard, or impossible, over a long period of time, but it's also going to generate, some might say, superficial kinds of things. Take the iPhone for example – is it creative? Creativity has always been market implicated. It's not like it hasn't been – look at Michelangelo's commission-based works – but what I argue is different, is that product development is driving the current definition of creativity. It's fine that creativity is decoupled from 'The Arts', but it's quite different to be hired by Apple to develop a product, than it is to be Michelangelo and say, 'Would somebody pay me to do the Sistine Chapel?'. They're both deadline based, but one is for higher work for profit. The iPhone brief isn't 'make up something really cool', it's 'make up something really sellable' – it's a completely different purpose. By virtue of design, today's definition of creativity will support certain kinds of development and choke out others. There's a lot of stuff happening in AI and VR (virtual reality) development for instance, but it's not always good for everyone. It's fun and it's interesting, and definitely profitable, but even in funding terms, investors behind 'creativity' research like ours are really looking for the innovations. That's part of our picture right now, but it's also not the whole picture. I'd love to see someone doing mindset shift work with corporates or schools around wellbeing – how can we do these things, but also feel like we're being kind to ourselves?"

The headline here? Achieving creative, 'personally sustainable' ways of innovating, working and living, will be an increasingly important line item on our #FutureFIT agenda, so take it on now to get ahead tomorrow.

In the zone: optimal environments for 'free-flow'

As an inherent communicator, both by trade and brand, there's no surprise my career has involved a hefty share of writing assignments served up with super tight deadlines. Journalist or not, however, today's climate of hyper-connectivity and productivity demands exceptional output from anyone operating in the professional arena.

I've long been curious about the conditions that have fuelled my most creative days. The days, hours and moments where I've felt utterly in the 'zone' – that divine place of utopia where I'm pumping out the goods with such efficiency and speed, I barely know I'm doing it. We've all been there. You feel unstoppable – you're onto something truly original, captivating and, well, at times you forget you're even working. You're flying! Was it the Pilates class you did that morning? The extra cup of coffee? The luxuriously deep sleep you had the night prior, or maybe your favourite Spotify playlist buzzing in the background? As it turns out, it could be a little of all of those things combined.

Baba Shiv, marketing professor at Stanford's Graduate School of Business, studies the neural structures at play in decision making and economic behaviour. The biological roots of creativity have fascinated him for some time. According to Shiv, creativity resides at the intersection of two primary pathways in the brain. Along the first pathway, the neurotransmitter serotonin governs whether you operate from a sense of calm and satisfaction, or anxiety and fear. On the second pathway, dopamine moves you from boredom or apathy, to excitement and engagement. Our best creative work is fuelled by a neurochemical cocktail high in serotonin and dopamine, producing a condition in which we're calm, but full of energy.

Try this at home... exercises in creativity: Part 2

I've always been partial to a G&T myself, but this ultimate creativity cocktail sounds like my new nirvana. Optimising our creative output is an imperative only set to accelerate in the years ahead, so how do we achieve this Zen-like 'zone' more often?

In essence, it all comes down to establishing the conditions for free-flowing happy hormones, and removing the triggers for the cortisol that counteracts them. Here's a bunch of tactics well worth building into your #FutureFIT plan.

1. Minimise stress in the office

Spikes in stress hormones such as cortisol counteract the creativity-boosting effects of serotonin. Furthermore, when we're stressed out, we tend to be closed off to new ideas and ways of doing things. When we're under immense pressure, we crave familiar people, ideas and executions; which sure smacks of someone likely to get 'stuck in their ways' and left behind!

Build it into your #FutureFIT Toolkit

Reducing stress in the office is no mean feat, but the benefits in store make it impossible to ignore. With the vast majority of employers now embracing flexible work for their staff, be sure to take stock of what environments and schedules work best for you. Do you work best among a buzzing team of colleagues, or in the solace of your kitchen table? Chances are your body, brain and soul will crave a bit of both, depending on your required outputs and associated deadlines. The trick is to take control of the situation – the era of 'face hours' is dead and buried, and heck, nobody likes a martyr. Lead by example and work smarter, not harder. And when you find yourself in a state of overwhelm, voice your situation to your manager or a trusted colleague ASAP. The sooner you flag the issue, the better your chances of correcting course to set yourself up for less stress, and more success. Speaking up is *not* an indication of weakness, but a marker of maturity, ownership and responsibility in an era that demands it.

2. Deep, deep slumber

Poor sleep can also have negative effects on creativity, and while we've all been well schooled in the almighty requirement of eight hours shuteye per night, the latest findings suggest it's the intake of deep, non-REM sleep that matters most. Our brains need up to two hours of deep slumber to restore adequate levels of serotonin. This sort of sleep accounts for less than 30% of the average person's slumber, and can be easily compromised by sleep interruptions, and consumption of stimulants such as alcohol and caffeine.

Build it into your #FutureFIT toolkit

Serotonin levels tend to be highest in the morning, making it an optimal time to schedule creative pursuits such as brainstorming sessions, spitballing strategic ideas and blue-sky thinking. To make the most out of the morning's elevated levels of serotonin, experts suggest swapping carbohydrates for high-protein options to start the day. Quite simply, proteins from a brekky like this are converted to much-coveted serotonin and dopamine. And for those wondering about their morning coffee? Caffeine acts as a physiological arouser, with the tendency to magnify whatever emotion you're already feeling. Headline: if you're 'in the zone', have another cup of coffee. If you're stressed to the nines about your afternoon presentation, skip it.

3. Get your blood pumping

The pitch here is simple: heart-rate-raising exercise enhances the neurological conditions for creative thinking by releasing a peptide that helps produce serotonin.

Build it into your #FutureFIT toolkit

After a nine month regime of Pilates to start the day, I'm an overwhelming advocate for morning exercise and its benefits to personal productivity thereafter. So much so, that I can't imagine ever breaking the habit. Challenge yourself to becoming 'a morning person' – if even for a daily 15 minute brisk walk around the block – and I promise you'll reap the creative rewards almost immediately. Afternoon meetings? Take a 10 to 15 minute walk beforehand or, better yet, suggest a 'walk and talk' session with your colleague or team instead. There are no rules here – optimising output is the only goal that matters.

4. Spice up your (intellectual) life

Maintaining a variety of intellectual interests keeps our creative juices flowing. According to Shiv, it's important to talk to people in other disciplines and read widely outside your field to develop "knowledge nodes" – bits of unrelated information that can come together to produce an unexpected solution. Indeed, Steve Jobs was renowned for this. His wide-ranging interests allowed for a creative lifetime of connecting the dots!

Build it into your #FutureFIT toolkit

Do you recall the brilliant benefits of 'forced adaptation' we learned about in Exercises in creativity: part 1? The argument for diversifying our interests and our personal skill-set beyond those we absolutely 'need' to perform our primary job function, is compelling. In the spirit of creative optimisation, feeding our brain with a diverse array of stimulants will produce the richest returns. Diversifying our 'brain food' can be done in an exhaustive and exciting, number of ways: through our consumption of content, our hobbies, our physical environments (say helllooooo to sabbaticals in unfamiliar destinations) and the types of people with whom we choose to engage (note, there's plenty more goodness on this last element in the next chapter!).

Go for broke: shake it up, then do it all again... and again... and again.

In closing, I'll leave you with Associate Professor Harris' brilliant advice for those looking to lead truly #FutureFIT organisations and teams:

> "There's enough literature out there now for leaders to understand which things worked, that seem to work, and those that don't, but the most important thing is to remember that they're all temporal and contextual.

"At Pixar 15 years ago, to roll in ping pong tables and have beers was really radical – the frictional conditions for creativity were present, but now you try to jerry-rig that and it has a very different feel – it kind of doesn't work. People are used to it – once it becomes formulaic, it's kind of dead. My advice would be to work with experts in the field to create frictional environments that encourage shifts in thinking and feeling. Let's paint some walls, change the furniture, reschedule the day, shift the defaults and talk across departments instead of creating silos (the enemy of creativity everywhere). So there's things we know, but then *you actually have to change*. And it's scary to change because there's a lot on the line, but if you really want to achieve great creative things, you can't just take a list of tips and affix them to your current status quo. You have to change multiple elements in your practice and environment, and keep doing it, and commit to doing it. Go back every six months and shake it up again."

Perhaps then, emotional regulation isn't *always* what we need when it comes to creativity. Harris explains:

"I think creativity is completely about 'emotional unlocking', risk-taking and sometimes very importantly, excess. Unfamiliarity and strangeness is the friend of creativity, and that's the commitment that I don't see – continuing to be precarious is stimulating, and it does create new solutions or problems, as it were. Keep changing! We have a default to the familiar – culturally, age-wise, for profit-related reasons – but if Pixar and Google can afford to engage in productive risk-taking when there's *that* much money at stake, then we can all afford the will to change too."

6

Actively networking

"Show me your friend-of-a-friend – and I'll show you your future." —DR DAVID BURKUS

Traditional networking is over. The future of work will require our networks to go deeper and go three-dimensional.

This does not mean rapidly increasing the number of people we know, by reluctantly walking into a room full of people we don't know and painfully collecting business cards. The 'new networking' will not be transactional. It will be about working within our existing network to establish meaningful connections and reconnecting with 'dormant ties' – for example, people we went to school with but perhaps have not spoken to for years. It will also be about being more intentional around the types of connections we lean on. It will be about cultivating a tribe that is connected, candid and caring. This will be far more efficient in the future of work when we look at how we'll be interacting with others.

Fifty-nine per cent of hiring managers using 'flexible talent' anticipate the work delivered by this emerging segment will increase by 168% in the next 10 years. So, as more professionals join the movement under alternative workplace arrangements, where they're hired on a project-to-project basis, landing work will be far more dependent than ever on who we know and how genuine those relationships are.

Everything old is new again

When I consider how I landed the most valuable piece of work in my business, I think about Candice Treloar. One of my oldest neighbourhood friends, Candice and I routinely spent Friday and Saturday nights together as teenagers, often scrambling for enough money to meet our girl squad in Surfers Paradise. We didn't go to school together, but we lived near one another, and were part of a local group of girls who were well rehearsed in visiting nightclubs well before we were legally allowed in.

Candice reconnected with me 25 years later, in the run-up to an event that I was facilitating in Melbourne. As it is in so many cases, it felt as though no time had passed since we were giggling and ordering cheap cocktails. But here we were, at a very grown up function where I was teaching women how to communicate with authority. Candice got so much out of the event that she referred me to work for her business, which turned out to be Telstra. Of all the work CareerCEO has delivered, that particular standalone contract remains the most valuable.

By definition, my connection with Candice was dormant – for over 25 years. And with that one reconnection, I was trusted to be introduced to an entire network of people in the supply chain department – a segment of the telecommunications giant that I would never have considered approaching.

Hidden power: old ties, new opportunities

What happened with Candice is a terrific example of what the research shows: that tapping our existing ties – the ties that go *way back* – is where the hidden power lies for all of us.

In a US study, 244 executives in four MBA classes were prompted to reconnect with contacts who they had not been in touch with for three years or more. They were encouraged to use those conversations to get information that could be useful to them for work. The results were a 'bonanza', with that information being in many ways more efficient than their everyday connections.

This strategy will no doubt resonate with any normal person who believes in quality over quantity. "The biggest wins come from reaching out to old friends. Because those people are in different circles now, different industries and different places – they provide the same new information and new opportunities as total strangers would, but it's easier to build rapport with them because they are literally your friends," says author and networking expert Dr David Burkus.

It makes perfect sense, right? Let's face it, once we leave school, university or any early jobs we've had, it's easy to lose touch with people who we've shared that experience with. It's not deliberate – life just gets in the way. And have you been to a school reunion 10 or 20 years along? It's hard not to have fun and be filled with utter delight when you see how your old buddies are spending their time. Dormant ties, these are the true assets in our network.

The 'new networking'

What a relief this is because, let me be bold: networking sucks. No one likes to 'work a room,' to promote themselves and extract opportunities from strangers. Not even extroverts – *not even extroverts love to 'work the room'.*

Not even extroverted former television reporters like it! Hitting up ten strangers a day was completely routine for me as a reporter – and while I got used to it (because repetition builds confidence in any task), I always felt a sense of dread alongside it. In those circumstances, I was usually extracting what I needed without the benefit of really 'giving back'. When there is no equal value exchange in the mix, it's an empty feeling. Sure, I got to meet thousands of people, but I always evacuated the context knowing that I had contributed nothing. It was a one-way trade. This is why traditional networking leaves us feeling a bit, well, dirty. Taking from strangers will do that to you. And how often does it actually pay off? These might be a few reasons why it's so hard to network, because the ground rules are straight-up unappealing to most normal, humble people.

So, how wonderful to know there's a paradigm shift for the term 'networking', in favour of a far more meaningful definition. The US research mentioned above can firmly redefine networking for us. The 'new networking' involves making real connections and having real conversations. It's not about adding more people that are similar to the people we already know, it's about understanding the network that we are already a part of and being active within that. This is technically known as 'social capital' – the value in our existing network.

As Dr Burkus says, the 'new networking' is about knowing "who is a friend and who is a 'friend of a friend'". Burkus believes that we have hidden networks that can transform our lives. How relieved are you already at the thought of mobilising the network you *already have* to seek out specific opportunities and create more diversity – in lieu of walking into a room full of strangers? I'm in!

The truth about networks

Let's be clear, people with well-developed networks have advantages. Let's laundry list them:

- They have access to more information, resources and market intelligence.

- They have access to emotional support that enhances wellbeing in times of change.

- They are better able to influence others.

- They are better able to get ideas off the ground.

- They are more likely to hear about job opportunities.

Think about how you landed your last three jobs. Did the door open to them via a recruiter, online search or advertisement? Or did they present themselves via a colleague, or a colleague of a colleague? The simple act of talking to people in our network leads to gain in some form. Maybe it's market intelligence, perhaps it's the scoop on a change of management or a genuine opportunity to get an initiative up and running. Social capital is real – it's the value in an existing network. We know that companies whose employees are loaded with social capital dramatically outperform their competitors.

Who's got your back? The 3D network

If you have a full-time job, I'm tipping that you've probably never had the time to consider mapping your network to determine the strong or weak ties, those who are considered 'influencers' within a business or where your gaps are. This is a fast and very revealing exercise that can help determine any action around your network, and provide a window to analyse the strength and diversity of your network.

To optimise our success in the future of work, we need our networks to go 3D. We need to be more intentional about the people who we associate with, spend time with and attach our brand to. This is *not* about being strategic or using people, it's about being purposeful about your relationships.

The version of networking that I find useful is one where we recognise who in our network:

- provides opportunity
- helps us learn
- is there to support us.

Let's take a closer look at what I mean by 3D.

1D: The breakout network

The people who can help you hit a target, land a job, raise money, land clients, get a book published – these people are your 'breakout network'. These are the individuals who will open doors, advocate for you, introduce you to the network that you need and who will make those critical connections that are outside your zone. They will help you break out of your current situation and into a new one.

Exercise #1

Think about one goal you'd like to achieve this year. Scan your LinkedIn network and write down five to ten people who can open a door for you that will lead to the goal.

2D: The schooling network

Who is going to help you learn what you need to learn to hit your target? They are the people in your schooling network. As well as teaching you what you need to know to be successful on the way to getting there, they will carry on teaching you once you arrive – supporting your continuous learning.

Exercise #2

We all need people to learn from, to reach our objectives, and this is where this particular shortlist comes in. When you look at your goals, write down five to ten people who you believe you can learn from in relation to these. Who's already mastered the job or skill you're going after? Who in your network knows someone who knows how to play the system, has the institutional knowledge or knows where the 'soft' power lies in an industry?

3D: The enforcement network

Who in your crew won't let you fail? This group could be as tight as two to five people. This is your enforcement network – those around you who will kick you into gear, follow up with questions and stay on your case when you're changing course or setting new objectives. These are the people who will hold you fully accountable.

Exercise #3

Take into account what you're going for and consider who truly takes time to listen without judgment, provides candid advice and will not back away from conflict. Think about who is not afraid to confront you about your ideas or plans. Who is comfortable having hard conversations with you?

Write down three people who are tough enough to hold you accountable, to call you out and who will chase you down to seek an update about where you're at with a goal.

Strengthen your network: five friends you can count on

Every major business has a body of elected or appointed members to oversee the activities of the CEO, but why wait to be a running an organisation to engage the support of an expert professional team? When I started my media training business in 2012, I created my own personal 'board of directors' to provide oversight, drive growth and help me manage tricky issues as I navigated the first few critical years in the marketplace.

Let me step you through who is on my board and the distinctions between each member.

Advisor

An advisor is someone who is hands-on with the tasks you are required to deliver. This is the person you ask off-the-record questions, for example: *"Can you tell me how to pull together my first slide deck for the board?" "Can you tell me how to structure my television news report?"*

So, do you have a list of people who are your go-tos for advice? Even if you do, I'd like you to write them down and think of a meaningful way to connect with each. Remember, people don't like being used. I bet *you* don't like being used. People don't like transactional exchanges, so what can you take to them to demonstrate your interest in their work and earn their attention? Make sure that you respect their time but also give something back.

Mentor

A mentor is a person with whom you can be completely candid. There should be no filter here when you talk to them. They get the backstory and the real version of events. You need to be able to say, *"I really stuffed up that presentation. It didn't land well with the audience, let me tell you exactly how it played out. How* can I rebuild my brand in the coming months?" Or, *"I've been offered an overseas posting, who should I call to find out what the team there is like to work with?"*

When you meet with a mentor, you need to feel as though they are prioritising you. Should they be inside or outside your business? We all need both. A mentor needs to understand your context so when they give you advice it's relevant and tailored appropriately. However, I also think there's a great advantage in having a mentor who is blind to the internal politics that you're facing, so you can hear advice that is neutral and objective of your context. A diversity of opinion will help you see a situation from all sides.

If you are assigned a mentor in a workplace, it's likely that you are both strangers, so consider them on probation! Over time, if you build up trust, that relationship may turn into a mentoring relationship. A mentoring relationship should be sincere and develop organically over time.

Sponsor

If they have complete confidence in your ability, a sponsor will run a mini-campaign for you. They will actively lobby all the right people on your behalf to appoint you into that new role or award you with that overdue pay rise. We can do just fine with mentors and advisors, but we won't necessarily go anywhere without being actively sponsored.

Connector

A connector makes change happen through people. They galvanise people. These are people who always have the right person to connect you with, once you've been specific about what you need. They love connecting people, so find this person for your 'board' and make sure you show your appreciation for who they bring into your life.

Curator

This is the person you can turn to for the real dilemmas – not just in business, but life dilemmas. It's someone you can trust with every kind of concern. This is a standout relationship because of three elements: vulnerability *(I can be my true self and know I won't be judged)*, sincerity *(I can put everything on the table)* and accountability *(I know they will follow up)*. A curator 'gets' you at a core level.

My career change curator

When I started considering an exit from my television career, I knew it was going to be significantly disruptive. (The term 'disruptive' turned out to be a wild underestimation of the years between 2010 and 2015. Is there a term for putting your life in a blender, blowing it up and starting from scratch?) I also knew that this would be a real shock to everyone who knew me. I decided when I was about 12 years old that I wanted to be a journalist – I wasn't exactly quiet about my goals, so everyone around me was part of that journey.

So abandoning my career was a massive call, and I wanted to consider it for a year before I told anyone or suddenly showed up in Iraq working for a humanitarian aid agency. I wanted to make the transition in a way that made sense to people around me. I wanted to be a story that continued to include everyone on my journey. My curator in this case was my long-standing friend from school, Sara Yates, who had worked across LA and London in high-performance roles in the film and marketing industry before moving back to Brisbane.

Here's some background to Sara. She had earned my lifelong respect during a nasty and unprecedented reputational disaster in Year 12. I was unceremoniously stripped of my prefect and house captain badges in front of the entire school assembly for skipping school on a day when – unbeknownst to me – my mother Judy was on tuckshop duty and found it unusually weird that I was absent from requesting free donuts by morning tea. I was across all the details, except the tuckshop roster.

I was busted and it was a very big deal to everyone but Sara, who approached me for the first time to give me her candid take on the drama that was playing out over months in front of the entire school community. At assemblies, in chapel services and other gatherings... in classic and predictable private school style, the principal took an unreasonable number of opportunities to make an example of me. To the point where I received supportive phone calls from mothers and teachers who told me to 'hang in there'. I still remember who offered those kind words through a phase where I was feeling unfairly defamed. Sara, wearing an above-the-knee, second-hand uniform and with her hair down, was a walking rule-breaker. "Mate, *so what* that the principal demoted you? SO WHAT? No one cares about this outside of that front gate."

Sara's blindingly objective view pulled me out of the private school scandal vortex, forever. This shift in my perspective liberated me from the approval-seeking that unconsciously drove the decisions of many around me. I no longer cared about what anyone thought from that moment on. Sara had recently been expelled from another school, and St Hilda's was her last chance after being rejected from Miami State High. Thirty years on, she is top of the list in my mobile phone category of 'favourite numbers'. Sara is the original curator. She is always listening in surround sound without judgment. Sara is the sanctuary and the situation room.

In an amusing turnaround, I was asked to be the keynote speaker at a St Hilda's luncheon in 2012 (20 years after I graduated) where a new, progressive principal officially reinstated me. He handed back my house captain and prefect badges and publicly apologised for the ordeal.

Returning to my career soul-searching... I sat down with Sara for a few hours, ran the scenario by her and asked her what she thought. She backed me without hesitation. The motivation and the move was a natural progression to her. And it really was. As a reporter I felt like I would parachute into a crisis, cover it and then scramble back out of there. I was particularly impacted by the suffering of others and I wanted to do more. As an aid worker, I *could* do more. That was the reason for the transition. And it's the thread that has run through my entire career, regardless of what I do: it's always about growing people. I bet you have a similar thread – while the function can look different to the outside world, the purpose is consistent.

Sara held me accountable, made suggestions and roused me on when I needed it. A curator is someone who's not afraid to offend you. They'll take you on, every part of you, never avoiding conflict and always having your best interests at heart.

Find your tribe

Networking is in our DNA. We are hard-wired to co-operate because it makes us feel good. And here is why we need to be more intentional about it in the future of work. We're used to living in close-knit groups where survival is dependent on one another, but author Sebastian Junger says today's society is just the opposite: in modern society, there is no guarantee that we're going to receive help and care when we need it. He says the divisions are getting worse, which prompted him to write the book *Tribe*.

As a journalist embedded with a group of soldiers in Afghanistan, Junger wanted to understand in detail the dynamic of tribes and what was behind the staggering rate of post-traumatic stress disorder (PTSD) in returning veterans. Junger's first war as a journalist was Bosnia between 1992 and 1995. He returned 20 years later to surprising insights. He found that civilians who survived (even those who had been injured) missed the conflict. They told Junger that during the war they had experienced their better selves. They were more concerned about others, they had been more generous and more courageous. They lived communally in the basements. They shared food. They were thinking about others as much as they would think about themselves. They missed the incredible generosity of spirit when the chips were down.

Junger says that our safety flows from being included. And modern society is so 'stable' that we don't need our immediate community around us to survive. While that's great in one sense, in another sense it takes away the chance for us to grow closer to those around us. This is why we need to be purposeful and intentional about building a tribe, particularly as technology will make it even easier than it is today to work alone and be alone.

Junger says the irony of modern society is that is does not bring psychological health. One study he references is a study that compared women in North America to women in Nigeria. The women with the highest rates of depression were the women in North America, which was the wealthiest group. Thus the women with the lowest rates of depression were the women in Nigeria. So how do we take the advantages of modern society and still have a close-knit society?

What Junger is saying is clear: we have to consciously create our own tribes and strengthen our networks. And when you're a part of one, you know. A powerful tribe has a strong sense of community; it lifts others, it's intimate, inclusive, caring, connected and candid. So, if you can feel yourself inadvertently slipping off the radar, or if you can see that others are: let your guard down. Open the gate, cut down the hedge (if you're fortunate enough to have one), throw open your front door once a month and host a dinner. Start building your own tribe and see it pay off. And be mindful of building a diverse tribe. As you look at the names in your network, how similar or different are these people from you? Are they similar or extremely different?

Let's stay connected and look after one another.

Start giving a shit: lead with generosity

"The sweetest and dearest word in the English dictionary is a person's name," said Dale Carnegie, an American writer and lecturer. As someone with a name that can occasionally be mispronounced ('On-drea') or easily confused for 'Angela', I get this to my core. Some people, who I have been introduced to, still call me Angela. Seriously, if you can't remember my name, I'm not inclined to help you out if you ever call on me. Don't be lazy. Remember names. Start giving a shit.

With the privilege of facilitating hundreds of people a year, I make sure there are name-cards in front of everyone and I always ask people with unusual names to spell them out when I meet them in other contexts. I really do give a shit. These souls have showed up to spend a day with me and I respect their time and their talent. If anyone follows up with me, I will often see their phone number and get on the phone. Aside from playing email tag and saving time, it signals that I simply give a shit.

Respecting those in your network is also about serving. This is why I encourage people to follow the Gary Vaynerchuk philosophy of 'Jab, Jab, Jab, Right Hook'. The New York entrepreneur wrote an entire book about how big brands can connect with their audiences on social media. There's a parallel here for individuals wanting to connect with their own audience. The rule is basically: give, give, give – then go in for an ask. "Your story needs to move people's spirits and build their goodwill, so that when you finally do ask them to buy from you, they feel like you've given them so much it would be almost rude to refuse," Gary says.

It comes down to service; by serving others sincerely, we'll be far more at ease asking for help when we need it. Some call it leverage – and yes, that's what it is. But it's not about keeping score. We want people we care about to be happy, so that's motivation enough to help out where we can. And when you can't help: say so. A few years ago I had a call from a friend whose daughter wanted to get work experience at Channel Seven News, where I had previously worked. There was no shortcut, I had to be candid. I told her that I would do anything to support the professional development of her daughter, *except* put in a call to the network. When I explained why, it made sense to her and she understood. So, when you can't help, say so. It will further the ties you have.

A footnote for my female friends

On a recent Tuesday morning, I breezed into the lobby of a major financial services building just off Circular Quay in Sydney. Running a few minutes early, I decided to join the queue for a third and very unnecessary coffee of the day. Scanning the jam-packed café, I noticed that out of probably 150 patrons, only about three of them were women. It was 8.50am, and there they were, across the lobby, scrambling towards the lifts to rocket up to their desks, log on and get down to business.

It was symptomatic of a gap we need to be hyper-aware of. The men were on the move, gathering intelligence, swapping notes and doing deals… while our female friends were bypassing the action because they're simply overly conscientious and concerned about not been 'seen' at their desk at the right time. Women should care less about the rules and spend more time walking the floor, catching people for coffees and hitting up managers above their paygrade. Show them something original. Hand them an initiative. Find another revenue stream for the business. Abandon the time-wasting mass gatherings where you pay up to $190 to sit next to the same person for two hours. Seek out real people and have real conversations that get real results for all involved.

If there's one thing I have vastly underestimated through my career, it has been building more 'slack-time' into my weeks. I experimented with this recently. For an entire month, I blocked out every Tuesday and booked in coffees with colleagues who I hadn't seen in some time. In every single case, from a free-flowing conversation with no agenda came work: new training gigs, from every meeting. That's a startling return on investment. It's tested and measured: slack-time is a sincere strategy for staying connected with friends (and friends of friends). Now, grab your diary and get out there.

7 Redefining leadership

"Leadership isn't hard – we've just been trained for years to avoid it. Don't be afraid to get into trouble. Don't worry about upsetting the boss. Leadership is up to us."

—SETH GODIN

The future of work needs a new wave of leadership. We need to be leaders who are original, entrepreneurial, bold, decisive and willing to make a ruckus. The urgent-scrambling emergency digitisation of business is bringing with it comprehensive and systematic restructure. The traditional workplace environment is morphing into a looser and more liberal form where teams are going remote, 'nine to five' is over, and so is the traditional style of leadership that thrived inside of those hours. We're seeing more remote teams working separately but collaboratively with greater flexibility around our lives.

And it makes sense. Instead of being on a manufacturing line, we've shifted to knowledge work, where everyone inside a business contributes to the revenue, culture and intellectual property of the company. The office is emptying out. Large segments of this knowledge work can be done from anywhere, so a new, fast, flexible and fluid employee model is gaining traction. An entire new set of workplace arrangements are replacing the safety net of being a full-time staffer.

According to a 'Freelancing in America' survey conducted by Upwork and the Freelancers Union in October 2018, the US freelance workforce is up 3.7 million people to 56.7 million since 2014; a growth rate of almost 7%. That translates to more than one in three (35%) Americans now in an 'alternative' work arrangement. By comparison, the non-freelance market grew 3% in the past five years from 103 million to 105.3 million.

Inside this extraordinary transition, there is a considerable problem – conventional leadership becomes lost and confused. What got us here, won't take us forward. Traditional models of leadership won't have anywhere to land in the new environment, and when we consider the way many leaders are being schooled, most MBA programs are yet to redefine what leadership means in a much faster paced environment where management of remote talent and teams is the norm. So, we have managers defaulting to outdated norms while simultaneously not being supported by anyone role-modelling the new modern brand required.

While the fault line is clear, so is the opportunity. Leadership for the fourth industrial revolution will require new simplified principles and a new level of 'bold' as we question and lead teams through a new narrative, in both big and small ways. Leaders who can't pivot will be pushed out, making way for a new type of executive.

A slow-mo exercise in leadership

My body was upside down but my head still managed to tip forward in slow motion, bringing my eyeline to lock onto the seat belt. It was more than a seat belt: it was a harness, with four points of restraints. All I had to do was hit the centre release button and I was free. But my brain was paralysed. I could see that my hands were relaxed on either side of the double-locked buckle, but I couldn't corral them to move. The harness that was created to save my life was now, apparently, a death trap.

Sacred seconds were ticking over. Sharpening my focus in the salt water was tricky. I was strapped into a helicopter that had just ditched into water, flipped over and was now sinking. Until the cabin stabilised, we were trained to stay put. In this case, that meant enduring a genuinely disorienting 180 degree turn. Taking a shallow breath as the water rinsed around me, any oxygen I had left was about to expire.

Staring at the seat belt, my brain continued to attempt to tell my hands to simply release the belt so I could open the door and swim to the surface. It should have been as instinctive as picking up a cup of coffee, but the neural pathway was blocked. Shock had set in. There were four people behind me and even in the silence of the underwater, I could sense the commotion behind me as someone presumably opened the passenger door to allow the group to scramble out of the wreckage.

For me, this emergency exercise was going unexpectedly wrong. I was in the front left-hand side of the chopper, with a very capable Air Force pilot sitting to my right. Out on the edge of the pool were three rescue divers who were clearly preoccupied with other members of the group – or perhaps, just not paying enough attention to the only person not showing signs of wanting to live.

I turned to the pilot and drew a blank. Nothing was registering, not even the ability to look panicked and summon his help. He could see what was happening. He was about to exit the aircraft, but turned around, snapped the latch of my harness, grabbed my right arm and dragged me out to the surface. It probably happened within two seconds but felt like everything was in slow motion, probably because that's how slowly my brain was moving.

As a news reporter for a capital city newsroom, part of my job was to routinely scramble into a helicopter to cover any kind of story. One day we might be hovering over a bushfire in unbearable heat, the next day we'd be covering an ocean rescue, gathering aerial footage of an overturned boat or – if it was a great day – sweeping across the Opera House to cover the annual Sydney to Hobart race. To be qualified for such days, however, a current HUET (helicopter underwater emergency training) certification was required. While primarily for medical rescue staff and anyone working on an oil rig, a very realistic simulator training exercise was also carried out for reporters in full reporter clothing – heels included.

As the daughter of a pilot who flew both light aircraft and helicopters, this should have been fairly routine. When there was any chance of a story that involved the chopper, my hand typically shot up. I grew up flying and was 'all-in' for any time in the almighty flying machine. Such comfort with aviation was the reason I was so deeply shocked at my utter lack of capacity to perform the third emergency drill that day.

In the moment, I didn't think much about what that pilot did for me, but as I reflected on the detail across the following year, things crystallised. When we were briefed, my understanding was that it was every man for himself. The entire point of taking part in such an intense emergency drill was to be tested, to be stressed to the absolute max, and to survive using your own individual awareness. When you signed up, it wasn't with your own crew, so there was minimal tendency to help out others in a way we typically would out 'on the field'. This wasn't an exercise in team-building. It was a pure play in building individual skill. There were instructors deliberately yelling as the aircraft was lifted by a crane and dumped into the Olympic size pool. The chaos was intentional.

Lucky for us, there was no leaking diesel in the water (imagine trying to breathe or see with that) or floating debris. Again, it was every person for themselves – except for the pilot next to me. He could have so easily left me there and let the rescue divers do their thing. That was, after all, their job – to recognise who was in trouble and intervene. But it was the guy next to me who came to the rescue. He could see I was in trouble the second we started sinking. Even in my genuine panic, I sensed that his head was angled ever so slightly down to the left. Perhaps I was invisible to others, but not to him.

Many years along, I'm relieved to know that this exercise is one that even experienced rescue pilots dread. Jerry Grayson, a 30-year veteran rescue pilot in the UK Royal Navy (and recipient of the Air Force Cross) told me that despite having 10,000 hours up at the controls, taking part in this crash training exercise, is "an unbelievably intimidating experience". Grayson holds the record for being the youngest person ever to join the Royal Navy at 17 years of age. His career outside the military has involved flying helicopters for high-octane action sequences in James Bond movies and leading helicopter crew teams to broadcast coverage of the opening ceremony at the Athens Olympic Games.

> "It's fascinating to find out something about yourself in situations like this. None of us ever find out that our brain is connected to our hand until you have to do it, so the advantage of finding that out in a training situation rather than real life, is hugely valuable. That is the purpose of the drill. And it's that compounded set of experiences that help you lead through moments of chaos and in some cases, helps to save your life and the lives of others."

Leadership: choose your own adventure

Until my HUET incident, I had always been somewhat confused about leadership as a young professional. I knew I was surrounded by adults who were 'more important than me' in the standard hierarchical sense, but they always seemed quick to disregard my ideas in favour of the status quo. The leaders I was exposed to throughout my early 20s went out for long lunches, offered little guidance and left me inherently disrespectful and suspicious of authority. I had wonderful mentors and sponsors, but struggled to find a leader in a newsroom whom I respected.

In hindsight, this likely explains my pursuit for growth which hit full swing in my late 20s, when I decided to relocate myself to Washington D.C., with no job, money or anything resembling a plan. It was a massive gamble on my own growth, but it seemed far smarter than waiting around to be assigned to a foreign bureau. Standing in that queue behind every other reporter would have meant waiting 10 years minimum, with no guaranteed return. Reaching my potential required a set of inspirational managers of a different kind. I was in the market for a non-conformist school of leadership.

And what a payoff. Seven years of working in and around the White House, State Department and Pentagon exposed me to extraordinary levels of leadership and human capability. I routinely conversed with, and interviewed, people who woke up every day to serve the nation or the community in ways that left me without words: families of 9/11 victims; wounded soldiers undergoing rehabilitation at Walter Reed Army Medical Center in Bethesda; scientists at NASA; the former Director of the Federal Emergency Management Agency (FEMA), James Lee Witt; Oprah Winfrey; and the first woman to be appointed Chief Scientist of the US National Oceanic & Atmospheric Administration (NOAA), Sylvia Earle, to name a few. Life changing conversations with the real deal makers and policy challengers left me inspired to my core, and motivated me to make a difference, if on a far smaller scale.

In a world overwhelmed by information and uncertainty, what does leadership today truly look like? We all need, and deserve, to find our own definition. It must be clear to us, in order to genuinely role-model it in our day-to-day lives.

To me, brilliant leadership looks like the aforementioned incredible minds, and my personal rescue pilot: those sharp enough to scan vast, chaotic, dynamic and often crisis-stricken environments, while remaining acutely attuned to what is unfolding immediately under their nose. To me, a leader isn't someone who toes the line, or believes he's above the minutiae. A leader is someone is who present, purpose-driven, paying attention, invested in the growth and progression of others, and who can make decisions in the moment, even if it means upsetting the boss or the board.

So, for those of us progressing through our careers, how do we become relevant, dynamic leaders, and what pragmatic principles can we adopt in the process?

Modern leadership: four simple operating models

In the traditional corporate structure, there is no clear distinction between 'leading' and 'managing'. If you're the General Manager at a bank, the expectation from your teams and the CEO is that you're doing both. That said, it must be recognised that leading and managing each require a distinct mode of operating.

"We have to be clear about what we're doing and communicate that with our teams," says Dominic Price, a recovering accountant turned Work Futurist for Australian software enterprise Atlassian. "Leading and managing are two different skills. If we're leading, let's be clear about that and get out of the road.

When we're managing, we need to make sure that everyone knows that as well."

So, if we're leading, how can we be more effective and make sense of the overwhelming amount of advice on the subject? Jonas Altman, Adjunct Professor at UBC Sauder School of Business and founder of Social Fabric, simplified this for us. Whether you're well on your way to the top, starting out on a graduate program or kick starting your own business, Altman's four-point policy is grounded in a default of 'what's best for the team?'. By adopting any one, or all, of Altman's four approaches in the right context, we ignite a multiplier effect – we create leaders who create great leaders.

Thank you, Mr Altman, for cutting down the spectacular volume of noise around leadership to the following four modes...

The Teacher

The Teacher focuses on leading and educating by example. By distributing authority to team members, she champions transparency, knowledge sharing, continuous learning and feedback. As four-star General Stanley McChrystal puts it: the interplay between leaders and their teams is a case of 'eyes on, hands off'. In other words, the Teacher stays acutely aware of what her team is up to and how to best support them, but doesn't meddle for the sake of it. This mode of leadership is entirely dependent on trust. And treating workers as competent professionals is something we can, and should, measure. This was the bedrock for the rich company culture that Patty McCord cultivated at Netflix – simply treating people as responsible adults made them accountable, empowered and engaged.

The Learner

As industrial systems grow even larger and more complex, leaders must develop new expertise on the fly in order to pull the right resources together, at the right time, and from across departments. 'Learner' leaders are conduits, synthesising and applying information – providing a key intersection along information paths. Tim Casasola, organisational designer at the theready.com, is a good example of a Learner. He helps Fortune 500 leaders adapt to the new world of work. That requires a mind open to continuous education, not only for employees, but for himself. "It's easy to fall into an outsider mindset," says Casasola, "But I remind myself I'm not the person with all the answers, I'm just someone that's there to help facilitate change – one they might know more about than I do."

The Mobiliser

The Mobiliser is acutely aware of organisational needs. As new information emerges from different and sometimes far-flung teams, it's the Mobiliser who responds with enlightened choices, bringing others into the fold to prompt collective action from the team. As a fresh-eyed CEO of industrial con-glomerate Alcoa, Paul O'Neill spent much of his time listening. He decided to put all his chips on the table and focus on one thing: safety. He encouraged all employees to regularly share information about worker safety. They did, and gradually started sharing all sorts of other information – including ways to boost efficiency and productivity. The focus on one item caused a domino effect across the business. Alcoa became one of the first companies to use an intranet, catapulting it light years ahead of its competitors. O'Neill's safety culture had com-pletely transformed its business. Alcoa witnessed a 5X increase in net income and a US$27 billion market capitalisation.

The Giver

Softly spoken, selfless, a big collaborator and an all-round nice guy – these are not the characteristics you would typically expect of someone at the helm of one of the world's largest companies. Yet that's exactly what Sundar Pichai is known for as the CEO of Google. His management style is pretty darn simple: helping others succeed. Pichai typifies the Giver who thrives in the new economy. Organisational psychologist Adam Grant explains that in stark contrast to Takers, when Givers succeed, something extraordinary happens: it spreads and cascades. Not surprisingly, companies that foster a culture of giving report more profitability, efficiency and customer satisfaction. And when a leader has Giver qualities it also helps to attract top talent and lowers turnover rates. Givers play the long game. While Takers might win 100 metre sprints, Givers win gold in marathons.

[Reprinted with permission from: Four models for a modern leader, Jonas Altman, *Quartz at Work*, May 4, 2018; and www.jonasaltman.com]

Trust me: I'm a television reporter

As team structures shift from 'mothership' to distributed models, each leadership model requires new levels of trust. This is a core imperative for the vast majority of leaders I engage with across corporate Australia. For these executives, trust is the currency of the new economy. However, what many of them struggle with is how to establish it with increasingly mobile workers, and how to empower their teams to embrace the autonomy that comes with more distance from the office.

When PwC Australia was equipping its staff to embrace 'the era of agile', they cleverly brought trust into the conversation early, and in ways that made it hard to ignore. One example was creating an internal podcast frontlined by prominent media personality Charlie Pickering. Pickering was engaged to interview people from within and outside the firm, who had proven experience establishing trust with remote teams.

I was one of the interviewees engaged for this project. Before PwC Australia contacted me, however, I had never once considered the concept of trust and how it played so critically into my role as journalist 'in the field' engaging remotely with HQ back in the office. Under this model, some work days were very local, while others spanned three time zones. The mechanics of trust, however, were constant. After chatting with Charlie, I reflected in great detail about how trust represents the very foundation of an entire news operation, how it works, and why it works so well. There was a simple, linear framework that we followed for every assignment. And it was seamless – based on the premise that the 'right' people are in place.

The right people in the right place

Let me state the obvious: having the right people on board is everything. I must acknowledge here that the operation of a newsroom is particular, in that its key performance indicators are blazingly transparent. If you miss a target, a million people will know. If you get a fact wrong, it's the same deal. Prepare for humiliation on a national scale. Prepare for Twitter outrage and phone calls direct from the viewer to the news director (which are logged and recorded to reinforce the learning). There is no place to hide and no excuse that softens the magnificently embarrassing blow of getting it wrong. In the news game, if you don't deliver, you won't survive.

Even on the worst days, any experienced news reporter who is on the road still delivers extraordinary levels of initiative, problem solving, adaptability, motivation, leadership, networking and curiosity because these are the absolute minimum skills you need to meet a deadline ahead of the competition. There is no room for passengers, and there is no room for frauds. Reporters are checked every day by the audience – and if we fail, we don't get to come back to work. Quite simply, we're politely (and sometimes not so politely) 'redeployed' to off-air duties.

Switching gears into the corporate world, I've been frequently awestruck by the volume of people who remain in a job they don't particularly like or feel is not the right fit for them. They deliver, but at times (in their own words) they've even told me they 'only strived to be average'. They suffered, the productivity of the department suffered and ultimately so did morale. To reiterate this principle of trust, I'll replay the headline: having the right people in the right job is non-negotiable. After all, how can we build trust with someone we know 'plays their role' because it simply pays well, or offers security, rather than it being 'on purpose' or aligned with their personal brand? In this regard, the first priority of a leader is to hire on right, and have the courage to fire on wrong.

A framework for trust

The following is a chronological blueprint of how a breaking news story plays out and how a news crew operates. For the purpose of demonstrating the framework, I'm sharing an example given to me by long-standing colleague Cameron Smith.

On 11 March 2011, Smith was the Supervising Producer for *A Current Affair* when an undersea magnitude 9.0 megathrust earthquake struck 70 kilometres off the Pacific Coast of Japan. Minutes after the earthquake struck, while the show was live to air, the host Tracy Grimshaw was physically being passed notes to update the audience. The earthquake had triggered an astonishing tsunami that wiped out hundreds of towns, leaving 15,000 people dead and thousands missing.

As a reporter, sometimes I think it's hard to be really shocked by a news event, because you're exposed to so much tragedy and, often, a significant volume of pictures that are too shocking to be broadcast. This story was next level, like the 2004 tsunami, the pictures coming in live to the newsroom were outright distressing. You know it's a huge story when the newsroom is quiet, because even the most seasoned professionals are startled by the reality.

This is clearly an extraordinary example but, as you will see, it shows how powerful a very simple framework can be when followed to the letter. The following framework can apply to any team, be it operating in the same location, or in various time zones. It's a simple, shared leadership model where everyone is invested in the outcome and, therefore, has a voice in the process. The 'lead' who champions the mission inside and outside the team, is the journalist.

1. Breaking news

A story breaks and the Chief of Staff (COS) decides if, and how, it will be covered.

In this case... The fourth largest earthquake ever recorded hits Japan while *A Current Affair* is live to air in Australia. A decision is made to send four news crews to cover for four different television shows for the Nine Network.

2. Team assigned

The COS identifies the reporter and camera crew. Roles are clearly defined (producer, reporter, cameraman, sound man) and although the buck stops with the journalist, there is no sense of hierarchy when a crew is on the road. Everyone is heard and decisions are frequently consensus driven. If a decision is overruled, it is usually by the COS and usually because they have new information to act on. The safety of the crew is paramount and every decision is guided by the best outcome for the audience.

In this case... Because of the significance of the story, a joint decision is made by the News Director and Executive Producers to send two crews on the next flight to Tokyo, plus one crew from *60 Minutes* and one crew from the *Today* show. Smith trusted that whoever his camera crew was, they were packing all the right gear – just as the crew knew that Smith himself was scrambling for any information to hit the ground running.

Smith meets the crew at the airport. "The best and most successful journalists are those who take a collaborative approach. In a highly unusual and dangerous situation that is developing, you're in it together, so having the crew's ideas and input is critical. If you're putting someone in danger, they want to, and should, have a say in how we're covering the story," says Smith.

3. Project assignment

The COS assigns the task clearly with the specific output required. The goals are shared by every team member.

In this case... The assignment was to cover the story any way possible. The crews are automatically empowered to do what needs to be done to get to the scene, which includes free rein of company credit cards and the responsibility of carrying camera gear worth hundreds of thousands of dollars. The crew lands and gets a train as far north as they can. They talk a taxi driver into hiring a minibus, which becomes home for the next five days.

4. Effective communication

The ground rules of information exchange are established and made clear.

- **How:** By mobile or SMS depending on quality of the coverage.

- **When:** When a crew arrives at the scene, or every time there is a development of any kind.

- **Who:** The reporter is the main point of contact, however the crew car phone number is dialled from the COS's desk, should they have any new instruction or information.

- **Purpose:** The purpose of communication has to be clear. Any confusion or ambiguity from the field risks the 'desk' losing confidence in the team's ability to assess the situation.

In this case... On touchdown in Tokyo, it takes 18 hours for Smith and the crews to get to Sendai. In that time, one call is made to the news desk to update.

5. The 'let-go' moment

Then, it's time for the COS to 'let go'. On any given day, they have four phones and two radios making consistent noise, plus 12 other crews to manage and the news production desk asking non-stop questions about what material is coming their way. The incredible thing about news is that nothing gets to air unless every single person delivers in their role. It's truly a team effort, with every individual contributing equally. The COS takes an 'eyes on, hands off' approach – they won't call or interfere unless there is sound reason to do so.

In this case... "We were there for almost three days, sleeping in the minivan, rationing petrol, eating out of vending machines. I got a call telling me that the nuclear reactor was going to be a threat. We had to evacuate the area because of the risk of it going off. No ifs or buts, we had to leave immediately. We implicitly trusted this call and followed the directive. Just as the COS trusted us to hotfoot it out of there to safety," says Smith.

Smith has since stepped out of the news game to run a Melbourne-based creative agency, Enthral, which employs

25 people to create content for top brands including McDonald's and Mercedes Benz. Smith reflects:

> "In retrospect, I've never seen trust play out the way it does in a news crew. There's no training for that. The trust goes in all directions between colleagues and it is unquestioned. Often, you're in volatile situations that demand heightened levels of awareness, which in a sense means everyone is looking out for one another equally. If one person fails, we all do as a team."

Shifting to a new paradigm

The essential nature of news gathering means that power has to be decentralised and shared equally among the team. The COS and all editors on the production desk know that a high performing news crew operates best when they're allowed to do what they do best. They can move faster and make better decisions. Effectively, everyone inside the building gets out of the road and stays out of the road, and the output (the news bulletin) is a product of what the crew delivers. High performance teams need to be left alone.

As a leader, the COS will only intervene if there is reason to. On a few occasions I've worked with a junior COS who lacked confidence in their decisions, and the impact was immediate. The second that confidence is lost, it's game over – news crews talk among themselves and to the production desk. Decisions are slowed down and second guessed, leaving everyone feeling exposed, vulnerable and questioning the quality of the final product. What I've learnt is that trust is both built and lost, in very small windows, in the minutiae of moments in which hesitation or doubt sounds in the voice of the person on the other end of the line.

As a news crew heading to a bushfire, violent protest or emergency scene, a big part of feeling safe or protected is knowing that you have an expert COS who is 'eyes on but hands off.' If they hear that conditions are deteriorating, you know they'll make a call to pull you out. Trust is firing in all directions. When debriefing after a big story, the COS will happily explain why particular decisions were made; empowering us with wisdom, context and detail to improve on our own.

The organisational structure of a newsroom is a compelling example of what we're seeing more and more across the corporate landscape: power being deliberately decentralised and with that, the disassembling of traditional hierarchies. "If you don't already have a culture of delegation and decentralised decision-making, now is the time to build one. You're going to need it when your team sits in different time zones," says Atlassian's Futurist, Dominic Price. "The most successful companies I've worked with are the ones where leaders recognise that 90% of the time, the best people to make a decision are the people closest to the work it affects. By contrast, companies where leaders hoard decision-making authority move at a snail's pace and (surprise, surprise) can't hold onto talented people."

It's a shift that is being embraced by more organisations. According to PwC, businesses are placing more emphasis on individuals and interactions over processes and tools. They are putting customer collaboration over contracts and are now responding to change as opposed to following a plan. They're organising their workplace in new ways with flatter, more dynamic structures; they're adopting agile methods like scrums, tribes, squads and sprints; incorporating other philosophies and approaches like Lean Thinking, Six Sigma and Kanban and they're collaborating using digital tools that bridge cities, countries and continents.

The future is a team sport

If we're able to let go and trust our teams, the payoff is tremendous. As Atlassian's Dominic Price puts it:

> "Most organisations misuse the word 'team' to mean department or function. In the Atlassian world, we use the word team to say the cross-functional people that you work with to get the same mission complete. It's not who you report to and it's not the political stakeholder engagement – where you go around to every single person to get their point of view and then placate them – it's saying, laterally who do I need to collaborate with to make this a real thing? It's more important who I work WITH and less important who I work FOR."

Price says that when you have that realisation, it frees up a ridiculous amount of time to work with your peers on getting the work done.

> "You get faster and you learn more. When I go and hang out with Sam and Kelly from Marketing, they take me out of my comfort zone, those are skills I'll never have. When we work together, that's complementary, versus when I hang out with my boss, we talk a lot about the same thing, that's homogenous and I'm not learning as much. To value the lateral stuff, you have to get over yourself because the insecurity of most leaders is, they look up, and in looking up they always think they're going to learn from above. I learn from my graduates, I learn from my peers and I learn from people above. If you're only going to one well, you're going to get thirsty."

Tenacious advocates for a thriving, dynamic workplace culture, Atlassian openly shares its **framework for successful teams** on its website. These are the ground rules for turning good teams into amazing teams, whether co-located or distributed:

- **Shared understanding:** The team has a common understanding of the problem they're solving. They're confident they have what they need and trust each other.

- **Full-time owner:** There is one lead accountable for results, and who champions the mission inside and outside of the team.

- **Balanced team:** The team has the right blend of people and skills. Roles and responsibilities are clear and agreed upon.

- **Value and metrics:** The unique value in the team's work is understood. Success is defined as a measurable goal that both the team and stakeholders agree on.

[Reproduced with kind premission from Atlassian Pty Ltd. atlassianteamplaybook.com]

This model is, in principle, the rule in play for newsrooms. As a former reporter, I can see how this translates so brilliantly to a corporate environment. When the right people are in place, this model builds astonishing efficiency within a business. Price adds that, "While team health is important for co-located teams, it is absolutely vital when you go distributed. Problems – whether with the work itself or with team dynamics – are amplified by distance."

Culture (in brief): a guide for change

Former rescue helicopter pilot Jerry Grayson remembers precisely when he understood why culture is so vital in moments of challenge and change:

"That came for me the first time I hung a nuclear weapon on the side of my helicopter. It's about knowing what team you're a part of, it's about understanding how far back that culture goes and part of that awareness of the culture is a feeling of not letting down the people who have gone before you. I was a naval aviator and reminded myself that Captain Cook was in his thirties when he discovered Australia. Knowing where you fit in and knowing that you do make a difference even if you're in a junior role. There's an element of understanding that the very fact that you're carrying a nuclear weapon means you're not just part of a four-man helicopter crew, you're part of 150 men on a squadron. All the way up to the Cold War. I just happen to be at the pointy end of the mission. It's the culture that gets you through it."

Now clearly, very few of us deal with a nuclear size issue on any given Tuesday, but Jerry's point is hugely relevant to all of us as we face the future of work in different ways. If we feel the work culture we're a part of is failing to guide us through an organisational transformation, routinely leaving us disempowered or ethically challenged, then the decision to stay and stick it out, or pack it in, is yours and yours alone.

My wish is that your #FutureFIT toolkit includes the ability to forecast whether a business (and the people running that business) has the capacity to create an environment which encourages respectful dissent from its leaders through times of change. If we're going to lead teams into and through a new era of work, we need to be shown the same modes of leadership by those leading us, as we're expected to offer to those around us.

Refining problem solving

"All great Acts of Genius began with the same consideration: Do not be constrained by your present reality." —LEONARDO DA VINCI

It feels like there aren't too many things that we humans agree on these days. One topic that opposes the trend is the importance of creative problem solving skills in the future of work. Everyone from Adobe to the New South Wales Government have commissioned reports on the importance of teaching problem solving. In the *Future of Jobs Report 2018*, the WEF gives problem solving double billing in its list of most in-demand skills (complex problem solving as well as reasoning, problem solving and ideation). As for time spent on problem solving, you can block out a third of your working week and colour it 'problem solving' by 2030, according to the Foundation for Young Australians report, *The New Work Smarts*.

These reports send a strong message: as automation assumes the routine aspects of work, we humans will need to ready ourselves (and our brains) to keep ahead of the processing power of algorithms. Predictable solutions won't be enough. We'll need to come up with new and innovative ideas that translate quickly to action to maintain a competitive advantage. That's why problem solving is an indispensable skill in your #Future-FIT toolkit.

There are plenty of problem solving frameworks out there and plenty of books devoted to explaining them. Here, I'll focus on the aspects of problem solving that I think make the biggest difference, no matter the framework. In particular, we'll look at what we as humans bring to the problem solving table.

There's no doubt creativity is important here; it's the electricity that powers problem solving and it gets its own chapter. But creativity alone doesn't make a great problem solver. #FutureFIT problem solvers combine the cognitive and social smarts to ask the right question. They read a room, encourage people who might be holding back from sharing and call out those people who are hogging the discussion. They then channel creative thinking quickly into action to offer a workable solution. In short, they deploy human skills to make themselves indispensable in the future of work.

A tale as old as slime

Consider a day in the life of an amoeba. It might seem strange to start a chapter on complex problem solving with a story about one of the simplest organisms on our planet, but bear with me. You might be surprised, our single-celled ancestors have more to say on the topic of problem solving than you might imagine.

Having evolved about 1.4 billion years ago, the daily routine of an amoeba is pretty straightforward as far as these things go. They find food, eat food and repeat. Assuming things go well, an amoeba might manage to grow big enough to reproduce. This generally involves splitting itself in two (a useful skill if ever I've heard of one). In some ways, it's an appealingly simple existence. But problems do pop up from time to time. What if there's not enough food nearby? It certainly complicates the find-eat-repeat routine. So what happens when these cells – which don't have brains or nervous systems – encounter such a problem? They solve it.

'They' is the key word here. These singular cells band together with others to form what's tantalisingly called a 'slime mould' and en masse go in search of food. Together, they expand and contract, sending out a network of tendrils which will surround any sources of food. Then they optimise that tendril network, narrowing it down to the key pathways that allow it to distribute the nutrients through the entire mass.

This behaviour has, of course, enticed scientists to test exactly what slime moulds are capable of. It turns out, if you put a slime mould at the entry to a maze and oat flakes (a slime mould's snack of choice) at the other end, the slime mould will find the shortest route to the food. Perhaps most infamously, slime moulds have shown that they can match it with the best engineers out there. When scientists introduced slime mould to a pattern of oat flakes that mimicked the placement of cities around Tokyo, the slime mould formed nutrient tunnels that recreated the shape of the Tokyo rail network. Bonkers.

Whatever it is that these brainless organisms are doing – and scientists don't yet agree on whether it could be called 'learning' or 'problem solving' – the results are the same. Slime moulds can compare options and make decisions. In effect, they are problem solving. Does this mean we big-brained humans aren't as special as we think we are? That's not what I take from this story. Certainly I rate my ability to find the most efficient route to good food, but I can also think about problems that are less immediately related to my ongoing survival. What I take from this story is that problem solving is part of what it takes to live in this world; it has been encoded in our DNA from our earliest ancestors and it has been carried forward through the aeons to today and will make us #FutureFIT for what comes next.

Outrunning the algorithm

As the slime mould story tells us, the importance of problem solving has been long recognised. More recently, it's entered the mainstream and for today's kids, problem solving sits right alongside reading, writing and maths as a foundational skill. The OECD Programme for International Student Assessment (PISA) first evaluated collaborative problem solving in its 2015 worldwide survey. In 2018, PISA went further and assessed students globally on the construct of global understanding, "the combination of background knowledge and cognitive skills required to solve problems related to global and inter-cultural issues."

If we needed more evidence of the importance that educa-tors are placing on problem solving, then the headline figures from Adobe's *Creative Problem Solving in Schools* report serve it up on a platter. Of the 1,600 educators (and 400 policy-makers and influencers) surveyed, 97% (and 96%) believed that students should learn creative problem solving skills. And 74% (and 76%) thought that these skills will be necessary for the age of automation.

For those of us already in the workforce, it's that last point that really gets us thinking (pun intended!). Certainly the lawyers and accountants and even the members of that seemingly most human of professions, the doctors, are starting to take notice. Wearing their white-collar armour, these professionals have always been untouchable. But sweat is beginning to build beneath those collars. Now, AI and machine learning are nibbling at the edges of these jobs and there's more to come. In *Jobs lost, jobs gained: Workforce transitions in a time of automation*, the McKinsey Global Institute found that current automation technology could happily snaffle 22% of the work done by lawyers, doctors, teachers, statisticians and chief executives. While first-year lawyers may cry with relief at the thought of outsourcing the drudgery of document discovery to a machine, AI is now also willing to take on legal research (among other tasks). Suddenly, those first-year billable hours are now looking a little grim.

This isn't the full picture, of course. As the title of the McKinsey report suggests, we're not just kissing jobs goodbye without welcoming new jobs through the door. Indeed, McKinsey's modelling indicates that the jobs lost can be offset by the creation of new jobs, assuming levels of economic growth, innovation and investment are favourable. The challenge is in the transition, ensuring that workers have the critical skills to make the shift from the way we have been and currently are working, to new ways of working. The new ways will be, at the very least, augmented by machine and will require graduates to enter the workforce at a sprint, rather than a dawdle. Ways that will therefore necessitate us all to level up our problem solving skills to become #FutureFIT, no matter what stage we are at in our career.

Frame it up

Most problem solving models out there begin step one with framing the question you need to answer. This makes obvious sense. The question shapes everything that comes after it: the data you collect, the people you speak to, the options you analyse and ultimately your final recommendation. But the right question isn't always the first question you ask.

Thomas Wedell-Wedellsborg, author of *Innovation as Usual: How to Help Your People Bring Great Ideas to Life*, explored this idea in depth in an article for the *Harvard Business Review*. Wedell-Wedellsborg surveyed 106 C-suite executives across 91 private and public sector companies in 17 countries. He found the great majority (85%) strongly agreed or agreed that their organisations were bad at diagnosing problems. A similar proportion (87%) strongly agreed or agreed that this flaw (surprise!) carried significant costs. He concludes: "The pattern is clear: Spurred by a penchant for action, managers tend to switch quickly into solution mode without checking whether they really understand the problem."

Writing for *Inc.*, Nicolas Cole puts it in slightly more Twitter-friendly terms: "This is what we like to call a BGO – a 'Blinding Glimpse of the Obvious.' In short: You're missing the right idea because you are focused on the wrong question." He adds: "Whether you are a lonely entrepreneur or a Fortune 500 company, it's not about finding 'the answer.' It's about taking the time to truly understand what question you are trying to answer."

Of course, a careful balance needs to be struck: time taken to properly frame the question is important, but so too is getting on with solving it. Running a complete Scrum cycle may be appropriate in some cases, but not all problems require this level of formal rigour. As Wedell-Wedellsborg explains, "The setting in which people most need to be better at problem diagnosis is not the annual strategy seminar but the daily meeting – so we need tools that don't require the entire organisation to undergo weeks-long training programs."

At the same time, Wedell-Wedellsborg cautions that applying simpler frameworks – like root cause analysis – often just digs deeper into the question as already framed. It doesn't challenge the premise of the question itself, so you'll still end up spending precious time asking the wrong question.

So far, much of the #FutureFIT discussion has turned on a need for speed, but investing time in framing might be an exception to this rule. It doesn't have to be a lot of time, but it does meaning taking a minute – or maybe 15 – to pause and take stock before again gearing up for action.

Problem solving in action: Framing

1. **Orient for action:** Nailing down the change you want to achieve helps to make sure that you've set the appropriate frame. To do this, create a headline question that captures the problem you're facing. Start with the words, "How do I..." or "What are..." to make sure the question is immediately linked to a particular outcome.

2. **Expand and contract:** Once you have your headline, it's time to test whether it's pitched at the right level – does it balance big picture thinking with the right level of detail? Do this by indulging your inner consultant and bringing out the flipchart or whiteboard. Write your headline question in the middle of your chosen medium. Use the physical space above your question to expand or explode your headline – why do we want to do this? Below, use the space to test if the headline is too broad – what do we need to do to answer this challenge?

3. **Phone a friend:** Bringing in different perspectives can help test whether you've framed the question appropriately. An easy way to do this is to simply try to explain it to a colleague who has nothing to do with the project. Explaining your thinking out loud helps to clarify the question and can uncover any holes. As a bonus, you get the benefit of input from another brain.

Diversity matters

How often do you hear about the importance of taking a cross-functional approach to problems? ALL THE TIME. You don't need a scientific study to tell you that solutions drawing on a diverse range of expertise are typically better than those created in siloes. Drawing on the full depth of organisational knowledge is an obvious way to make sure proposed solutions aren't too narrow and you're not missing easy wins. But in recent years, the research has been building around the importance of other forms of diversity. Gender diversity often grabs the headlines, but social, cognitive and neurodiversity are now equally important ingredients in the problem solving pudding.

Why *is* diversity so important? It certainly doesn't make group dynamics easier, introducing greater risk of miscommunication, increased conflict and lack of trust, among other undesirables. These perceived negatives arise from the different perspectives, experiences, social norms and opinions that diversity brings crashing together. And that is, of course, the point. From this melting pot of difference, more innovative solutions emerge.

In 'How Diversity Works', published in *Scientific American* in 2014 (and republished in 2017 in response to President Trump's stance on immigration), Katherine W. Phillips, Senior Vice Dean at Columbia Business School, reviewed the research on the link between diversity and problem solving. Her review makes a compelling case in support of, as the 2017 issue retitled it, why diversity makes us smarter. Phillips' analysis is fascinating because it reveals that the different information that diverse perspectives bring to the table isn't the critical point. It's the fact that interacting with people different from ourselves changes how we behave. Those behavioural changes lead to better decision making and ultimately better, more innovative solutions. As Phillips explains it:

> "Members of a homogeneous group rest somewhat assured that they will agree with one another; that they will understand one another's perspectives and beliefs; that they will be able to easily come to a consensus. But when members of a group notice that they are socially different from one another, they change their expectations. They anticipate differences of opinion and perspective. They assume they will need to work harder to come to a consensus."

Phillips concludes that this is how diversity works, it promotes creativity and hard work. It encourages us to look for and consider alternatives even before there has been any interpersonal interaction. She encourages us to think of the challenges of diversity as similar to the challenges of exercise. There's no pain without gain (as the cliché goes)! We need to push through in our teams, organisations and society as a whole if we are to "change, grow and innovate".

Problem solving in action: Diversity

1. **Do the hard work:** Most of us shy away from conflict, but as Phillips reminds us: no pain, no gain. When building a project team or consulting stakeholders, push yourself to bring in as many diverse perspectives as you can.

2. **Adopt a 'difference mindset' in every interaction:** By always interrogating your own assumptions and bringing an open mind to all discussions, you can consciously recreate some of the behavioural adjustments that we unconsciously make when working in diverse teams.

Collaborate... sometimes

Common wisdom is that collaboration is a great thing. So much so that collaborative software programs like Slack are now seen as indispensable, while today's offices are designed to promote collaboration in real life. So this may be a little controversial, but research suggests that being all in on collaboration all the time doesn't actually produce the best solutions.

In a 2018 study titled 'How intermittent breaks in interaction improve collective intelligence', the authors gave groups a standard problem to solve and then looked at the impact of the time spent collaborating on the quality and quantity of the solutions each group produced. One set of groups never interacted (always off), a second set interacted constantly (always on – sound familiar?) and the third set interacted intermittently (on and off).

Their findings had a distinct Goldilocks flavour: not too much, not too little, but just the right level of collaboration delivered the best result. While the always-off groups won the quantity prize, their overall quality was lower because these solutions included both the best and worst possible options. The quality prize went to the always-on groups, who came up with the best average quality of solutions, but they lacked variety and were less likely to come up with the optimal solution. The on-and-off groups showed it's possible to achieve the proverbial best of both worlds – the solutions created by these groups had the same average quality as the always-on groups, but by preserving individual work time, these groups also managed to come up with the most creative solutions as well.

The study had one other interesting finding, something believed to be entirely new: the highest performers were able to improve further by learning from the low performers only in the on-and-off groups. The suggested reason? When high and low performers interact constantly, the low performers basically copy the high performers and so, to put it bluntly, the high performers ignore them. But when they only interacted with the low performers every now and again, the high performers were able to take something away from these interactions that improved their performance.

The lesson from this study is remarkably straightforward: to generate the best solutions to a problem, balance team interaction with individual work. Job done.

Problem solving in action: collaboration

1. **Set the ground rules:** If you want to create a working environment based on intermittent collaboration, the best way is to be intentional about it rather than hoping it will happen organically. At an early stage, discuss how you can schedule interactions and individual work time. This includes how you'll use collaborative software. One option is the Scrum approach, have a quick daily stand-up to check where everyone is at and plan further work.

2. **Try a hackathon:** From the offices of Silicon Valley comes the hackathon, a dedicated event where people step out of their everyday jobs to come together and solve problems and develop new products. But programmers shouldn't have all the fun. A hackathon mentality can be used for any creative problem solving activity. These days tend to be highly structured, so use the structure to promote intermittent collaboration (as well as diversity).

3. **Make the best use of your physical environment:** Sometimes, the set-up of an open plan office can mean you end up in an always-on group by default. Think about how you can use the space to ensure that interactions stick to

the on–off schedule. If necessary, find your own space to create individual working time.

The vital importance of psychological safety

So far, I've discussed a range of powerful concepts that have proven to have positive impacts on problem solving. But none of these concepts will get you any closer to upgrading your #FutureFIT problem solver status alone. They have to be supported by a psychologically safe working environment. That is, people must feel like they won't be punished if they make a mistake. Where that safety doesn't exist, we risk activating our lizard brains – the fight or flight response – which may have served us well on the savanna but is not well adapted to the modern workplace.

Of course psychological safety doesn't mean that everything will be sunshine and lollipops all the time; I've already talked about how diversity can bring out more conflict. But it does mean that there won't be any personal ramifications for a bit of respectful (and figurative) head-butting. In fact, studies show that when team members feel psychologically safe, they're willing to take moderate risks and are more creative and willing to speak up. Sounds like a #FutureFIT problem solving paradise.

The willingness to take risks is particularly important here. The rapid rate of technological advancement, industry disruption and the adoption of new business models means that organisations must quickly iterate and prototype solutions to problems. This has to involve a level of calculated risk-taking as time no longer allows for every eventuality to be tested beforehand. Successful problem solvers must be willing to try things and if they don't work, they need to move on, taking their learnings into the next iteration.

There are plenty of tips out there on how to create a psychologically safe work environment: for example, creating rules of engagement; cultivating a growth mindset; building a constructive feedback culture. And all of these things are important, but I was interested in exploring a more novel approach. I spoke to Dr Kate Raynes-Goldie, multi-award-winning game designer and explainer of the future, about how engaging in play can help us problem solve in a safe – and fun – environment.

"Problem solving is definitely one of the skills that we can't necessarily automate yet, but who knows what's going to happen," says Raynes-Goldie. "So what I'm really interested in is how games and playfulness can actually help teach that skill."

It's clear we share a passion for empowering #FutureFIT leaders. Raynes-Goldie works with groups, from teenagers through to seasoned professionals, guiding them through an experiential learning process that explores rapid prototyping, iteration and user ethnography through play. It's this focus on playfulness – introduced by (wait, this gets a bit meta) making a game out of making a game – that promotes the feeling of safety and unlocks an increased willingness to just have a crack at things.

"I find that games and playfulness create this kind of magical space where adults, once they get into it, are willing to do things they wouldn't otherwise do," explains Raynes-Goldie. "They remember what it was like to be a kid, and it makes it safe and fun to do all these things that we don't need to be scared of because they're really, really important, like experimentation and failure."

Going through the process of designing a game becomes a way of teaching those skills. "It uses the same process as other problem solving," says Raynes-Goldie. "But by making it a game, you're making it safe and fun for people to try new things and build that into their problem solving skill-set. It's about making experimentation fun and safe."

She's not afraid to experiment with this approach in her own life:

"I would say basically everything in work and life can be looked at as a game. And I personally will play games with myself as a way of challenging myself to change my mindset or accomplish a goal. I ask myself: 'How can I frame this as a game?' An example is where I have the opportunity to do something in a day that scares me. As long as I'm not going to be in physical danger, if it scares me, I tell myself, 'This means I need to do it because it's going to teach me something.' When it becomes a game, it somehow makes it easier for me to do it, it's less serious and I'm not attached to the outcome.

"I'm actually really shy talking to strangers, so I played a version of this game that involves me talking to five strangers. Just having a non-transactional conversation. Like walking into a bookstore, standing in the philosophy section and just randomly talking to people there. And because it was a game, it just made it easier for me and made it a bit silly. Maybe I was awkward and maybe that person did think I was a weirdo, but that's OK because I talked to them so I won my game. So just think about how you can game-ify your life or game-ify your work so it's no longer a chore. Instead it becomes fun and a whole lot less scary."

Problem solving in action: Psychological safety

1. **Get playful:** Take inspiration from Kate Raynes-Goldie and think about how you can game-ify elements of your problem solving processes, both personally and in a team

environment. Personally, identify areas of your problem solving skill-set that you want to work on. For example, if you want to work on free brainstorming more ideas, set yourself a daily challenge to come up with 10 ideas for a particular topic. Keep a tally of your points. And a little retail therapy reward never goes astray too, if that's your jam.

2. **Put people first:** Some of the concepts we've discussed can start looking like tick-a-box exercises. Don't fall into the trap of simply consulting your go-to diverse colleague each time you want to broaden your perspective. The same goes for locking in collaborative time versus individual time. Cultivating psychological safety means respecting people as people first.

3. **Make an example... of yourself:** If you do make a mistake, own it and own up to it. Whether you're leading the team or not, role-modelling honest ownership can help shape a psychologically safe culture. Ask for and offer constructive feedback to improve and celebrate team wins rather than rushing on to get started on the next pressing concern.

Where we land is that problem solving isn't a simple cognitive process. I'd love to suggest that you start doing the 'Daily Mini' crossword in *The New York Times* every day and consider your work here done, but it's nowhere near that simple. (But by all means, do the crossword, it's definitely good for you – it's a stand-alone app.) Instead, we're left with the need to develop and deploy a complex set of social and cognitive skills that will help us navigate the many human interactions that lead from problem to #FutureFIT solution.

Embracing continuous learning

"The illiterate of the 21st century will not be those who cannot read and write, but those who cannot learn, unlearn, and relearn." —ALVIN TOFFLER, AMERICAN FUTURIST

Continuous learning **is** no longer an optional extra in our career toolkit, but a non-negotiable pillar in our #FutureFIT strategy. The relevance and power of our personal brand depends on it. As we transition between jobs, across sectors and between businesses, we'll need to upgrade our minds as frequently as our devices, in order to keep up with the market.

While automation, cloud technology, artificial intelligence and robotics are set to be adopted at different rates in different industries, the pace of transformation and innovation in general is picking up. In quantitative terms, 75 million current jobs may be displaced by the shift in the division of labour between humans, machines and algorithms, while 133 million new roles may emerge at the same time (according to the 2018 *Future of Jobs Report*).

New jobs, or modified jobs, mean new skills, and let's not forget the entirely new mobile workforce being engaged by organisations. Fifty three per cent of US businesses already have a flexible workforce in place. Remote workers and freelancers are up 24% from 2017, an Upwork report shows. This is a workforce committed to staying competitive, a workforce more optimistic than ever about the future of freelancing, and a workforce which values skills training over formal education. Most importantly, this flexible workforce is one dedicated to frequently upskilling to stay marketable – 70% of full-time freelancers invested in training in the past six months, compared to 49% of full-time workers.

For many of us, this emerging trend is an opportunity to start a new learning policy that will future-proof our careers. Look around your business, understand what new technologies are being adopted and how such changes will transform the organisation. Then, utilise these insights to map your own disruption. Not only will this help you identify new ways of working, but also to isolate new value-generating opportunities for the business. Once you've mapped your disruption, you'll be well placed to move ahead with a learning plan that both protects and prepares you for an ever-changing future landscape.

Above and beyond the business impetus, learning is transformative. It creates positive change in ourselves and our communities. Imagine moving from a traditional learning model to one with greater fluidity and flexibility. Imagine a learning model in which graduation isn't finite, but ongoing...

The lowdown on continuous learning

How many days of professional development or training did you log over the last 12 months? More than 10? Less than 10? Less than five? A straw poll of the CareerCEO alumni (mid-career professionals across corporate Australia and New Zealand) revealed most workers clocked between five and ten days total.

Holding down a secure job for a reputable organisation requires far more than simply showing up. It requires keeping up. However, if you've been coasting along performing your fair share of 'presenteeism' when it comes to professional development, upskilling and learning, then you'd better brace yourself for some confounding research. According to bold insights being shared by think-tanks like the WEF, our future of work will not only require showing up and keeping up but, in some cases, even catching up. In September 2018, the WEF released its *Future of Jobs Report* which declared that on average, employees will need 101 days of retraining and upskilling between 2018 and 2022. Yep, 101! That's an average of at least 25 days for each of us per year.

Emerging skill gaps among individual workers and senior leadership alike may significantly obstruct an organisation's transformation. Depending on industry and geography, a whopping 50% to 66% of companies are likely to turn to external contractors, temporary staff and freelancers to address their skills gaps. Jumping back to the fact that 53% of US businesses are already using flexible talent (freelance, temporary and agency workers) compared with three years ago, what mindsets are driving the shift? In the US, 42% say the main motivator is a more flexible schedule, but they equally know the trade-off is remaining competitive. Thus, continuous learning is embedded in their mindset. Incredibly, 51% of freelancers say no amount of money would get them to take a traditional job.

So a new and optimistic workforce is now penetrating the corporate arena at a rapid rate, they won't trade anything for it, and they're routinely upgrading their skills. And who are the individuals increasingly choosing to be part of this gig economy? They are professionals with the most in-demand skills. For young professionals with runs on the board, it's plain to see why shifting to a looser work arrangement is so appealing. It enables more time with family, the opening up of more creative opportunities, and no annual leave forms or process to endure.

Having personally freelanced for 80% of my career, I know it also comes with legitimate downsides: lack of stability, a reluctance to plan any holidays, unwelcome payment terms from big business clients of up to 90 days and, at times, a battle with the banks to get any kind of loan in line with your unpredictable income. For me, however, the long game perks of flexible work are truly unmatched. Over and above all of the irritants of the 'gig economy', the burning platform of mandatory continuous learning in order to land future work is perhaps one of my greatest loves. This isn't about competing against others, but bettering myself, meeting interesting new people, creating a tribe, performing tasks that require intellectual curiosity each and every day. What a gig!

Having said this, of course I appreciate everyone has their own rhyme and reason for working the way they do. I acknowledge we all have unique circumstances, pressures, wants, needs and risk profiles. When I boil it down, however, it's always the opportunity to learn that drives me to work the way I do. And now, as a teacher and provider of professional development training across the corporate arena, I'd like to see full-time workers granted more time to learn and more time to work flexibly – to come in a little later after school drop-off, or leave mid-afternoon to make school pick-up, or take an afternoon off per fortnight to care for an aging parent.

Rarely do I see businesses truly liberating their people with the time or space to submerge themselves in learning, even when a program requires two hours a week. I see schedule warfare everywhere, and I'm sure you do too. A plethora of competing corporate interests continue to place 'learning' behind back-to-back meetings, internal politics and overdue projects. Too often, training, learning and professional development programs are not taken seriously, and this demands action, urgently.

Sure, at times we've all had L&D providers who've left us jaded after failing to inspire, but when this happens, it's up to us to look further for someone who does. Forget about the digital divide, the future of work is about the motivational divide. It will belong to those who don't simply accept the changes coming their way, but actively pursue them. And yes, even when that means taking on a few extra hours a week, or month, to level up and keep up!

University graduation day: just the beginning

Rather poor planning by yours truly resulted in me almost missing my own university graduation ceremony. It wasn't a big deal until the day prior, when I somehow convinced my father to change course from a family holiday so I could walk across the stage, shake the hand of a stranger and collect a piece of paper. If only I had known that wasn't the only opportunity I had to graduate... I would have stayed on the beach, applied another layer of 50+ and made the most of the Queensland sunshine.

Since that day in 1995, I've collected a few more pieces of paper: a Graduate Diploma in Defence Studies, a Masters of International Strategic Studies, a Harvard Kennedy School executive education program, 'Women and Power: Leading in a New Era', and a Massachusetts Institute of Technology (MIT) course in 'Artificial Intelligence: Implications for Business Strategy'. There was a solid 15 years between the MA degree and the enlightening discovery of executive education.

This was an unavoidable hiatus. A demanding daily news cycle took over my life, until the day I walked past a news stand on K St in Washington D.C. en route to an 11am–11pm news shift at the Al Jazeera English bureau. It was a career changing moment in the most ordinary of routines. Instead of picking up *The New York Times* (which was my daily standard practice) I glanced at my Blackberry to see what was leading the US news agenda. It was March 2008. A few steps past the news stand, I stopped and looked back. I took a moment and realised that, unconsciously, I had just formed a new habit, and one that would lead me to abandoning my entire career in news.

I walked into the bustling newsroom observing my colleagues with a fresh perspective and slightly terrified eyes. As I logged in, the gravity of my new mindset started to seep deeper. I was a news reporter who wasn't watching the 6pm news or buying a newspaper. I was working exhausting 12 hour shifts, seven days a week. I had no 'plan b' and no other formal skills, no other experience working outside of the news business and now the business model of news was imploding – fast.

Much like putting on prescription glasses for the first time, everything around me became razor-sharp. Until then, I had really no idea the fog I was in. The following day I asked colleagues if they had ever thought of re-skilling to transition out of news, and I was thrown nothing but genuinely confused responses. "Why would I do that? I love what I do – as if I would ever need to change." Clearly I wasn't the only one flying naively through a sea of clouds. With a polite nod and subtle eye roll, I rapidly proceeded to upgrade my résumé. It was time to reboot my mind and transfer my skills to a different industry. It was time to think differently about learning; to establish a model that would help me continuously develop, remain relevant and maybe even start a business of my own.

School's out: an education revolution

A revolution in education is zooming down the pipeline and the voices supporting it are getting louder and more prominent. Progressive minds around the world are now observing the growing disconnect between the traditional school system and what young minds actually need in order to thrive in the real world.

In 2012, marketing icon Seth Godin delivered a powerful speech called 'Stop Stealing Dreams' about the state of US education. Godin's address offered a sharply scathing assessment of the traditional school system, noting its very design is intended for mass production and not for individuals. By this design, says Godin, school is about teaching obedience and compliance. "Why wouldn't we want our kids to build something interesting, to go figure it out for themselves? Are we teaching our kids to collect dots, or connect dots?" Among his eight suggestions for overhauling the system is lifelong learning, and celebrated 21st century philosopher Yuval Noah Harari is equally on board. Harari writes about the urgency of many issues facing humankind today, and how we can maintain focus in the face of constant and disorienting change. According to Harari, one of those burning issues is education. "By the middle of the 21st century, accelerating change plus longer lifespans will make our traditional learning model obsolete. Life will come apart at the seams, and there will be less and less continuity between different periods of life."

Our society seems to be obsessed with our kids going to the best school and then the best university, even if it leaves us drowning in debt for our early adult lives. But what then? What Godin and Harari identify is that all traditional learning systems are now outdated. We need to innovate the way we educate, and that applies to educating adults as well. The good news? Our timing is right on.

Modern learning: there's no back row

An unapologetic nerd, I'm a subscriber to daily updates from places like GetSmarter.com and the Massachusetts Institute of Technology, and when 'New Course' emails hit my inbox, I admit to feeling a disproportionate degree of excitement. When a girl living in suburban Sydney can access subjects like machine learning from her kitchen table, while simultaneously feeding local kookaburras, that's truly exceptional stuff. What's more, when the lecturers, instructors and insights are coming to you from the world's top ranked universities, everybody wins.

The democratisation of education is a phenomenal evolution for humankind – particularly for those who aren't keen, or in the position, to commit to a multi-year term, moving cities or parting with tens of thousands of dollars for the sake of an abundance of theory over practice. Furthermore, the opportunity cost of leaving the workforce for an extended period of 'study time' is financially impossible for the majority of us. Hindsight is always a beautiful thing, but looking back at my 'fast-tracked' two-year BA degree (which I reluctantly stretched out to three years due to failing subjects like 'print journalism production' and 'introduction to law') I can only cringe at the valuable time I lost in a classroom where the theory taught had very little to do with the practice. We now know we need both: the old (tried and tested principles, frameworks, methodologies and formulas) mixed in with the new. We need solid, proven foundations, yet we also need the pragmatic lowdown on how they apply to the real world. Then, and perhaps most critically, we need the capability to implement our ideas and insights at lightning pace; to connect the dots in real time and boast a willingness to constantly iterate and update our solutions on the fly.

If there's a term for an online-learning addict, I'll loudly and proudly wear the label. If there's a learning platform or short course you've been hesitating to try, then take it from me and our friends at the WEF – it's absolutely time to build it into your #FutureFIT toolkit.

By 2022, the WEF says that 54% of employees will require significant upskilling, and online platforms like GetSmarter. com are taking the forecasts seriously. Founded in 2008 by two South African brothers, the GetSmarter mission was to deliver better education and improve the lives of one million working professionals by 2030. The brand's first offering was 'Wine Evaluation' in partnership with the University of Stellenbosch. Later that year, the University of Cape Town agreed to collaborate, and today, GetSmarter offers programs from Oxford, Cambridge, HarvardX and MIT. Is it working? American EdTech giant 2U certainly thinks so, snapping it up from the brothers for US$103m in 2017. Nice one, gents.

4Line Learning model

Another leader in the modern learning arena is the Southeast Asia Center (SEAC) whose purpose is nothing less than transforming the quality, quantity and effectiveness of leadership capabilities in Southeast Asia. SEAC has developed a learning approach called '4Line Learning' in order to meet the learning requirements of each individual, while simultaneously addressing the participants' desire to apply their learnings to their life and work amidst a climate of aggressive change.

There are four parts to SEAC's 4Line Learning model. The first is 'Online Learning' which makes learning accessible anywhere, anytime, on any device. The second is 'Inline Learning' where learners are encouraged to take part in short, sharp classes and courses – half a day's duration at most. The third is 'Beeline Learning', underlining the value of experience and information exchange with experts, speakers and business leaders. The fourth part is 'Frontline Learning', where learners are granted full access to downloadable materials to guide their day-to-day endeavours in the real world.

A spokesperson for SEAC shared the following official statement:

> "We firmly believe that every human being must never stop learning and developing their life potential, and that they all want to create a positive change in themselves, their organisations and the society. Therefore, everyone needs to be aware and understand how to learn, unlearn and relearn with new mindsets especially amidst the world of Disruption. That said, SEAC strongly wishes that we could serve as an important centre for lifelong learning where everyone is allowed to think and shift mindset as well as create a Lifelong Learning Ecosystem in the society to reach the Learn Fast, Fail Fast and Move Forward culture. This is all for the advancement of themselves, of the organisation and of ASEAN's present and future."

Powerful stuff, and a policy that responds beautifully to any individual looking to ensure their learning integrates seamlessly into their greater life. Yep , that's all of us.

Intellect: the new currency

We know that knowledge is power, but I'd encourage you to think about it being even more. What if knowledge was currency – boasting more value in the market, and in our lives, than money itself?

According to a pool of 'master thinkers', one thing is for certain: learning is the single best investment we can make. Deliberate learning or deliberate practice is what we're referring to here. In a bid to understand more about how elite minds use 'deliberate learning', celebrated entrepreneur Michael Simmons (as recognised by the White House, Ernst & Young Entrepreneur Of The Year, Inc. 30 under 30, Businessweek 25 under 25, Bank Of America) shortlisted the world's over-achievers and invested a year in exploring their personal habits. Deliberate learning became a glaring pattern, with Simmons finding that great minds dedicated an average of five hours per week to learning.

For some, learning is built into their job. Take Captain Richard de Crespigny, who flies an A380 for Qantas. De Crespigny is required to practise specific skills in a structured environment. In one instance, he is required to be in the simulator practising a landing in a 20 knot crosswind. Such learning is termed 'Deliberate Practice' (DP), because it specifically targets a skill to improve on. De Crespigny goes further, asking for a 40 knot crosswind. He wants to be able to land at the maximum limits of the aircraft. Knowing that DP has a payoff, de Crespigny also pursues information from other pilots who have experienced failures of some kind.

On 4 November 2010, de Crespigny's compounding interest in learning paid considerable dividends, when he safely landed flight QF32 after a catastrophic engine failure. Captain de Crespigny's experience and leadership allowed him to avoid one of the world's worst aviation disasters on record.

Not everyone will have the need to target one specific skill, but the A380 captain shares a confounding pattern with leaders like Barack Obama, Warren Buffett and Bill Gates: they all prioritise time for learning. On top of a daily one-hour learning ritual, Gates even takes an annual two-week 'dedicated reading holiday'. That's one high learning bar you've set for us, Mr Gates, but we certainly like it!

In concluding his study, Simmons shared a poignant observation:

> "In short, we can see how at a fundamental level knowledge is gradually becoming its own important and unique form of currency. In other words, knowledge is the new money. Similar to money, knowledge often serves as a medium of exchange and store of value."

Note to self: Hard work is not learning

Here's a critical distinction: you might be working hard, but that doesn't qualify as learning. Sure, you might be super committed to your work, but that might provide diminishing returns over time. Learnings, however, will pay off far more exponentially. Don't confuse them, says Simmons: "Most professionals focus on productivity and efficiency, not improvement rate. As a result, just five hours of deliberate learning a week can set you apart."

Simmons has a simple directive around the subject:

> "Just as we have minimum recommended dosages of vitamins, steps per day, and minutes of aerobic exercise for maintaining physical health, we need to be rigorous about the minimum dose of deliberate learning that will maintain our economic health. The long-term effects of intellectual complacency are just as insidious as the long-term effects of not exercising, eating well, or sleeping enough.
> **Not learning at least 5 hours per week (the 5-hour rule) is the smoking of the 21st century so here is your warning label."**

Sign us up! The next step? Getting big business on board.

Try this at home: Create your own curriculum

You get the idea: embrace lifelong learning or risk being irrelevant. So how can we create a framework to organise continuous learning for ourselves?

I prefer not to be overwhelmed or lock myself into a program more than three months ahead of time (with an executive education program at Harvard Kennedy School being the exception due to the planning involved around cost and time out from work). Instead, I take my learning schedule one quarter at a time. Blocking out half a day at the start of each quarter (the first day of January, April, July and October), I'll take some time to think about what I'm curious to know more about, and how that might play into and strengthen the Career-CEO business at large. If they align, that's brilliant. When they don't, bizarrely, it can end up being just as valuable because my thinking becomes even more diversified.

Try these four steps to help you lock in ongoing regular learning as part of your #FutureFIT toolkit.

1. Set clear learning objectives

Be clear and directed when setting learning objectives. Drill down into what it is that you want to know, including why if it's more than curiosity alone.

For example: *I want to understand more about 'fintech' and the 'shared economy' that we're now part of, which starts with understanding the core principles of economics, fintech and the disruption facing the financial services sector.*

2. Combine old school with new school

Each subject has two parts: the 'old school' and the 'new school' content.

Old school: These are the fundamental concepts of the subjects. In this example: knowledge of financial markets, transactions, economic basics and so on.

For the old school fundamentals, I'll keep it traditional – go straight to a bookstore and browse through the 'Economics 101' books, of which there are plenty.

New school: These are the less foundational, and relatively new, concepts around the subject. In this case: shared economy, fintech, trends in 'proptech' (property technology) and 'regtech' (regulatory technology).

For the new school concepts, I might sign up to an Oxford University online course via GetSmarter.com (the Saïd Business School runs a fintech program). The course synopsis clearly states a commitment of 12–15 hours per week over 10 weeks. The reality is, I know zero about economics, so I'll personally need to extend the recommended investment of time to truly absorb the content – perhaps up to two full days per week. It's a serious chunk of time, so I'll block out two days in my diary now, and start planning around it.

Clearly, the old school, established principles set the foundations from which new ideas and concepts emerge. The reason behind 'old school' versus 'new school' classification isn't simply to organise the vast number of concepts to be learned, but to guide the sequence of learning those concepts. The sequence of our learning is crucial. Imagine being taught calculus before basic subtraction! For this very reason, old school concepts have primacy and the new school concepts flow from these.

3. Latch onto the street smarts

For me, latching onto 'street smarts' is where the learning magic happens. These manifest as 'soft' knowledge insights spanning any learning around the 'hard' facts. These are the moments when our understanding truly deepens, because we begin to form connections between ideas and theory. It all starts to crystallise: you can apply the knowledge in a new way, without supervision! Listening to a podcast, hearing a keynote speaker at a conference, even having a conversation with an expert in the field – these are all moments that further your understanding of a topic.

As a journalist, I've only recently been ready to acknowledge the awesome privilege it is to be in the company of leading scientists, biohackers, engineers, policy makers, business leaders and people whose work dominates their respective industries. The questions you're accustomed to firing go well beyond the basics, and the people on the receiving end are far more likely to be intellectually generous because they trust your genuine interest in knowing more.

One footnote to building the street smarts: industry conferences can be an exceptional place of learning, but you *must* allow time for the content and connections to settle. We're often deluged with waves of new, exciting and incredibly relevant information in these contexts – so much so, that we owe it to ourselves to block time *after* the event to make sense of it all, just as we'd take the time to revise first-time learnings from an executive education program.

4. Commit to your revision schedule

Admittedly, this is where I often go wrong.

After being an incredibly diligent student of a recent MIT program on the business implications of artificial intelligence (which demanded one full day of study each week for six weeks), I unintentionally let the weekly revision schedule slip, (not entirely, but I most certainly could have done more). This was a massive error of judgment; not only because the program included a show-stopping calibre of content, but because the alumni I had access to afterwards (650 brainiacs from around the world) were fully engaged and organising meet-ups to discuss the concepts throughout the active study window.

It's remarkable what happens when like-minded people sign up to learn more. They establish real connections through shared passions for learning, for personal development and for working out how it all applies in the big, wide commercial world. Next time, I've committed to being 'all in' on revision.

We all absorb learning differently, so we need to design a revision model that's best for us. One model is the Leitner system, developed by German scientist Sebastian Leitner, which is a simple process of repeatedly using flashcards. Personally, this system isn't right for me. Once I've written a summary paragraph about the content, however, my confidence in the subject really builds, even if it's 200 words, as if I'm briefing a colleague. This system of revision is certainly unproven and may only work for my brain, but my point is to encourage each of you to find your own way of revising critical content.

Once you've built confidence in your new area of learning, your expanded intellect will truly begin to add value to your everyday.

Endnote

My simple intention in writing this book is to get you thinking. Yes, the future of work means job displacement and disruption, but it also means innovation, career correction or an entirely new direction. Ultimately, the degree of friction is up to us – are we willing to shift our mindset to recognise real opportunity for our own growth, or are we going to sit quietly with the status quo and wait to see how it all plays out?

It's a game of initiative. And it's about mindset. But it's also about creating the space in our lives for the best mindset possible – for reflection, recovery, for potential change and making the very best decisions. I've taken years to understand that mindset, wellbeing and building our own resilience, are the baseline for handling any transition. Resilience is our ability to bounce back from a setback. We all deal with uncertainty in different ways, and finding our own baseline can stabilise our minds, offer calm in the chaos and bring focus.

Everyone has a different baseline anchor. For some it's yoga, for others it's running, reading or taking a daily walk. Sometimes it can be as simple as a sound. We recently had a noisy tide where I live. An east-north-east swell was meeting a south-westerly breeze, resulting in waves so big you could hear them a few streets from the beach. The salt in the air was so dense it was distracting. I usually don't open my eyes before my alarm, but on one particular morning, I was literally woken by the waves.

The last time I was woken by the ocean I was about 10 years old. My mind was utterly absent of anything to worry about except avoiding oversized frill-necked lizards in the neighbour's yard while legging it to the school bus with my sisters. That's why this recent morning was so wondrous to me. To be eased into an average Tuesday by the same daily backing track to my simple childhood without mobile phones, apps or iPads. There was no noise other than the waves, the neighbourhood kookaburras and the constant giggle of primary school siblings.

I now know the hum of the ocean is my own personal baseline – the backing track that has buffered me through every transition to date. It's why I switch 'ocean sounds' onto my sleep app when I'm taking risks, or experimenting with life far from home. It's how I put things in order. It's easier to go further when you know you can return to the comfort of a baseline, a community, a connection where you feel the happiest. Be sure to find yours.

Whenever I contemplate my future of work, I wholeheartedly take the opportunity to stand back, to look at the 'system', to figure out where I might fit in and where I'm able to contribute value and feel completely at ease. Through this book, I hope that by recognising and growing your #FutureFIT skills, you can take the time to do the same. What does your future of work look like? How do you want to live, and what is your personal baseline from which to build a life that allows you to be more connected to yourself, your purpose and your community?

Afterword

Finding your own Future Fit

There have been many books written about the future of work and no doubt there are even more in the pipeline. Depending on the author they'll all preach much the same message: namely, "the only constant is change". The argument being that we are living in momentous times and that today's workers are facing disruption on a scale unmatched in human history.

I don't believe a word of this shtick. Previous generations have indeed managed disruption on a grand scale. Consider for example the generation born in the 1890s in Australia. I'll call them the Federationists. As young adults they endured the globalisation and the horror of what they called The Great War. By the time they were in their late 30s the Federationists were navigating the effects of a global recession. And to top it off, by the time they were middle aged, say 50, their 20-year-old sons were drafted into World War II.

But that's not all; the Federationists also saw the shift from farm work to city factories, the shift from horses to motor cars, the advent of the telephone and the invention of the radio. They would have witnessed the horrors and the infant mortality of common viruses like measles and whooping cough, and even the simplest of things that we take for granted such as the sanitation of our cities via the development of sewerage systems.

And yet the Federationists survived. They prospered. They built a better Australia. They sacrificed, and they did what they could for their families. We humans are a remarkably adaptive species. But this book isn't so much about mere survival, it's about prospering. I have no doubt there were Federationists who struggled with their modern world. Yet looking back, those who seemed to prosper, who lived happy (even if humble) lives, seemed to me at least to be easy-going kind of people.

Those who were wedded to protocol, processes and to hierarchies never really came to grips with the 20th century notion of a rising middle class. I think the same logic applies in the early decades of the 21st century. We Australians will continue to be buffeted by global forces – not so much by war but most certainly by trade, immigration and technology. There are skills that every one of today's future-fit worker must have, such as completion of secondary school and some sort of post-school training in the vocational or higher education sphere.

But that's just the beginning. As Andrea so adeptly demonstrates in this book, you'll also need to have the ability to adapt, to marshal resources and networks, to occasionally be brave, really brave, to sometimes suck-it-up and just do it, to often make-do with inadequate resources, to surround yourself with smart and supportive colleagues and to continually learn new skills. But, there's more to learn yet.

Clarke's great skill, I think, is in being able to dissect a given situation, to break it down into its components, and to draw lessons and learnings from each bit. It's about learning how to project authority and confidence and it's about being sufficiently gutsy – bold – to call out inappropriate behaviour in those to whom you report. It's life-shaping, gut-wrenching and scary stuff.

There is no rule book in how to manage in the workplace and even less guidance on how to navigate a workplace being tossed and turned by forces over which you have no control. What you need in this topsy-turvy world is buoyancy, which might be described as the ability to keep bobbing up. Read

Andrea's account of her time in Washington D.C. or in Iraq and see how she handled each changing situation. Not perfectly, I am sure she would say, and not without personal angst and pain. But survive she did, and even more importantly she learnt from these often harsh and awkward if not downright unfair experiences.

Working your way through life, through a career, and especially in times of change, will never be smooth. You should expect, and you should welcome, stormy seas and that's because it is these turbulent times that separate the prepared from the unprepared. Make sure you're in the former category. Reading this book is a start.

Future Fit: how to stay competitive and relevant in the future of work sketches the bigger picture, provides real-life examples of how to navigate challenging times at work, and dot-points strategies to surviving and thriving in the workplace of the 2020s and beyond. It is a how-to manual, it is a series of real-life stories, it assembles evidence of the way the world of work is changing.

If there is one lesson from this book, it is the need for future workers to be able to see the bigger picture and to have the resilience and the grit to do what is required to navigate in the right direction.

Bernard Salt AM

Sources and index

Chapter 2: Building reputation capital

Botsman, R. (2017) *Who Can You Trust? How technology brought us together and how it might drive us apart*, Portfolio/Penguin.

Cho, YJ and Perry, JL. (2012) Intrinsic Motivation and Employee Attitudes: Role of Managerial Trustworthiness, Goal Directedness, and Extrinsic Reward Expectancy. *Review of Public Personnel Administration*, 32(4), 382-406.

Godin, S. (1999) *Permission marketing: turning strangers into friends, and friends into customers*, Simon & Schuster.

Grant, A, et al. (2007) Impact and the art of motivation maintenance: The effects of contact with beneficiaries on persistence behavior, *Journal of Organizational Behavior and Human Decision Processes*, 103(1), 53-67.

Harari, YN. (2018) *21 Lessons for the 21st Century*, Spiegel & Grau.

Kerr, J. (2013) *Legacy: What the All Blacks can teach us about the business of life*, Constable.

Sethi, B, Stubbings, C, Gratton, Prof. L and Brown, J. (2018) *Preparing for tomorrow's workforce, today*, PwC Global.

Sinek, S. (2009) *Start With Why: How Great Leaders Inspire Everyone To Take Action*, Penguin.

Sinek, S, Mead, D and Docker, P. (2017) *Find Your Why: A Practical Guide for Discovering Purpose for You and Your Team*, Penguin.

Wall, B. (2018) Brand Amplified.

Chapter 3: Sharpening communication skills

Anderson RC, Klofstad CA, Mayew WJ and Venkatachalam M. (2014) Vocal Fry May Undermine the Success of Young Women in the Labor Market. *PLoS ONE*. 9(5): e97506.

Nielsen. (2017) 2016 U.S. Music Year-End Report.

Pentland, A. (2008) *Honest Signals: How they shape our world*, MIT Press.

Vaynerchuk, G. (2017) The Rise of Audio & Voice. garyvaynerchuk.com

Chapter 4: Tapping into adaptability

Berg, A, Buffie, EF and Zanna, L-F. (2018) *Should We Fear the Robot Revolution? (The Correct Answer is Yes)*, IMF Working Paper Working Paper No. 18/116, International Monetary Fund.

Centre for the New Economy and Society. (2018) *The Future of Jobs Report 2018*, World Economic Forum.

Chua, R. (2018) The cybernetic newsroom: horses and cars, *Reuters*.

Crouch, I. (2015) The Sportswriting Machine, *The New Yorker*.

Davis, N. (2018) Exponential Technology Trends That Will Define 2019, *Singularity University*.

Dweck, C. (2006) *Mindset: The New Psychology of Success*, Ballantine Books.

Fratto, N. (2018) Screw Emotional Intelligence – Here's The Key To The Future Of Work, *Fast Company*.

Friedman, T. (2016) *Thank You for Being Late: An Optimist's Guide to Thriving in the Age of Accelerations*, Farrar, Straus and Giroux.

Goleman, D. (1996) *Emotional Intelligence: Why it Can Matter More Than IQ*, Bloomsbury Publishing PLC.

Goleman, D, Boyatzis, R, Davidson, RJ, Druskat, V and Kohlrieser, G. (2017) *Adaptability: A Primer* (The Building Blocks of Emotional Intelligence Book 3), More Than Sound, LLC.

Harari, YN. (2016) *Sapiens: A Brief History of Humankind*, Vintage Publishing.

McCrindle. (2018) Generation Z: Exploring the characteristics of the emerging Generation Z and Generation Alphas.

Mullin, B. (2015) How The Associated Press is using automation to rethink the way it does news, *Poynter*.

The New York Times. (1987) The Battle of the Spreadsheets.

Zaccaro, SJ, Gilbert, JA, Thor, KK and Mumford MD. (1991) Leadership and social intelligence: Linking social perspectiveness and behavioral flexibility to leader effectiveness, *The Leadership Quarterly*, 2(4), 317-342.

Chapter 5: Nurturing creativity

Adobe. (2016) *State of Create: 2016*, Adobe Systems Incorporated.

Beaty, R. (2018) New study reveals why some people are more creative than others, *The Conversation*.

Beaty, R. et al. (2018) Robust prediction of individual creative ability from brain functional connectivity, *PNAS*, 115(5), 1087-1092; published ahead of print January 16, 2018.

Centre for the New Economy and Society. (2018) op. cit.

Grant, A. (2018) What Straight-A Students Get Wrong, *The New York Times*.

Manyika, J, et al. (2017) *Jobs lost, jobs gained: Workforce transitions in a time of automation*, McKinsey Global Institute.

Spitznagel, E. (2018) Naked, Drunk, and Very Tired: What I learned from trying to live like a genius, *Medium*.

Stubbings, C, Williams, J and Brown, J. (2017) *The talent challenge: Harnessing the power of human skills in the machine age – 20th CEO Survey*, PwC Global.

Chapter 6: Actively networking

Junger, S. (2016) *Tribe: On Homecoming and Belonging*, Grand Central Publishing.

Levin, D Z, Walter, J, Murnighan, K. (2011) The Power of Reconnection: How Dormant Ties Can Surprise You, *MIT Sloan Management Review*, Spring.

Upwork. (2018) *2018 Future Workforce HR Report: How HR is preparing for the skills of the future*, Upwork.

Vaynerchuk, G. (2013) *Jab, Jab, Jab, Right Hook: How to Tell Your Story in a Noisy Social World*, Harper Collins.

Chapter 7: Redefining leadership

Altman, J. (2018) Four Models for a Modern Leader, *Quartz at Work*.

Upwork and Freelancers Union. (2018) *5th Annual Report: Freelancing in America 2018*, Upwork and Freelancers Union.

Chapter 8: Refining problem solving

Adobe. (2018) *Creative Problem Solving in Schools: Essential Skills Today's Students Need for Jobs in Tomorrow's Age of Automation*, Adobe Systems Incorporated.

Bernstein, E, Shore, J and Lazer, D. (2018) How intermittent breaks in interaction improve collection intelligence, *PNAS*, 115(35), 8734-8739.

Cole, N. (2016) Why the Right Answer to the Wrong Question Is Still the Wrong Answer, *Inc.*

The Foundation for Young Australians. (2017) *The New Work Smarts: Thriving in the New Work Order*, Foundation for Young Australians in partnership with AlphaBeta.

Lamb, Prof. S, Maire, Dr Q and Doecke, E (2017) *Key Skills for the 21st Century – an evidence-based review (Future Frontiers Analytical Report)*, New South Wales Department of Education.

Manyika, J, et al. (2017) op. cit.

Miller, P and Wedell-Wedellsborg, T. (2013) *Innovation as Usual: How to Help Your People Bring Great Ideas to Life*, Harvard Business Press.

OECD. (2015) *PISA 2015: PISA Results in Focus*, Organisation for Economic Co-operation and Development.

Phillips, KW. (2014, republished 2017) How Diversity Makes Us Smarter. *Scientific American*.

Wedell-Wedellsborg, T. (2017) Are You Solving the Right Problems? *Harvard Business Review*.

Chapter 9: Embracing continuous learning

Centre for the New Economy and Society. (2018) op. cit.

de Crespigny, R. (2018) *Fly!: Life Lessons from the Cockpit of QF32*, Penguin.

Godin, S. (2012) Stop Stealing Dreams, TEDxYouth@BFS.

Harari, YN. (2018) op. cit.

Simmons, M. (2018) The Founders Of The World's Five Largest Companies All Follow The 5-Hour Rule, *Medium*.

Southeast Asia Center (SEAC).

Upwork. (2018) op. cit.